MASTERS OF MUSIC

Beethoven and His Friends

MASTERS
OF MUSIC

By
ARVID C. ANDERSON
41710

Biography Index Reprint Series

BOOKS FOR LIBRARIES PRESS
FREEPORT, NEW YORK

STANDARD BOOK NUMBER:

8369-8012-3

LIBRARY OF CONGRESS CATALOG CARD NUMBER:

70-117320

PRINTED IN THE UNITED STATES OF AMERICA

Contents

Johann Sebastian Bach

Johann Sebastian Bach

1685-1750

The Musician's Musician

~

A LITTLE lad trudging along a country road approached an inn midway between Hamburg and Luneburg. He was footsore and hungry. The odor of cooking food tempted him to enter the inn, but alas, his nearly empty purse did not allow even another meal. Undaunted, he seated himself outside the inn to rest his aching feet and to muster his strength in order to resume the long homeward journey.

Suddenly a window of the inn was opened, and two herring heads were thrown in the direction of the lad. In each he found a Danish ducat, sufficient not only for a meal but also for another trip to Hamburg. Some kind person, sensing the plight of the little wayfarer, used this strange means of bringing assistance to him.

This was not the first time, nor would it be the last, that Johann Sebastian walked the twenty-five-mile distance between the two cities. In attendance at the convent school of St. Michael in Luneburg, he made frequent journeys on foot to hear the great Dutch organist, Reinken, of Germany's chief port city. The physical privations and discomforts attending these expeditions were forgotten in the inspiration and satisfaction that were brought to his youthful soul by the playing of the noted musician.

Born in Eisenach, near the edge of the Thuringian Forest, Sebastian lost both parents by the time he was ten years of age; whereupon his older brother, Christoph, who had married, assumed the responsibility of providing a home as well as an education for him.

That Christoph took his responsibility seriously is borne out by the restrictions he imposed upon his charge. Talented and trained in music, the older brother had acquired an important collection of organ compositions which he highly prized, insomuch that he refused Sebastian access to it. Sebastian, on the other hand, thirsty for the pure waters from the fountainheads of music, longed to embrace the precious volume.

One night when all the members of the household were asleep, he stealthily left his bed, and on tiptoe reached the latticed bookcase in which the precious book was kept. He managed to wiggle it through the latticework, and began to copy the music by the light of the moon. Night after night, whenever there was a moon, he assiduously copied the forbidden music by the same method until, at the end of six months, when the task was just completed, he was discovered by his guardian-brother, and the music was taken from him. At first thought it appears that Christoph's restraint was prompted by selfishness, or by jealousy of his younger brother's growing talents, but it is possible also that Christoph, having the ultimate welfare of Sebastian at heart, did not wish to overtax him with music beyond his years.

The trait of indefatigable purpose as shown by Sebastian in this incident was but one of the strong attributes which characterized the Bach family line. For several centuries the traditions of integrity, of piety, of devotion to family and to art, passed from generation to generation. As for music, it seemed to flow like royal blood through their veins.

No less than ten composers, fourteen organists, a dozen

musical directors, a number of court musicians, and many experts on orchestral instruments contributed to the establishment of the Bach musical dynasty. And then a prince arose among them, towering head and shoulders above his kinsmen, inheriting the accumulated genius of centuries, reigning supreme in the fields of creative and interpretative art. There would come the day when Johann Sebastian Bach's realm would include not merely a remote corner of Germany but the entire world.

At eighteen years of age Sebastian began his career as court musician at Weimar. Shortly afterward he accepted the post of organist at Arnstadt. While there, eager to study the style of the Danish organist, Buxtehude, resident at Lubeck, he obtained a month's leave of absence and made the two-hundred-mile journey on foot to attend the sacred musical performances over which the great organist presided. He outstayed his leave by three months, making it necessary for him, on returning to Arnstadt, to appear before the consistory to explain his extended absence, and further, to explain the appearance of a "strange maiden" in the choir. Doubtless the latter was Maria Barbara, who on October 17, 1707, became his wife.

Meanwhile, a vacancy in the organist post at Muhlhausen brought a new appointment with larger responsibilities to the young musician. The yearly salary was to be eighty-five guldens, twelve bushels of corn, two cords of wood, some kindling, and three pounds of fish. The expense of transporting his household furniture was to be borne by the parish. As the customary mode of transportation was a four-wheeled cart, drawn generally by a cow and a pony, it is supposed that this was the vehicle furnished.

Bach was an orthodox Lutheran and the pastor at St. Blasius was a Pietist; therefore it was not long before their conflicting views, especially in the matter of music's place in the religious service, effected an estrangement. So when a call was sent for Bach to fill again the position of court organist at Weimar, he unhesitatingly accepted.

Congenial surroundings, a comfortable salary, and mutual interests with his royal patron contributed toward making Bach's

nine-year stay at the Weimar court both pleasant and profitable.
Mizler writes, "The benevolence of his gracious sovereign inspired him to attempt all that was possible in the art of handling
the organ, and here it was that he composed most of his organ
pieces."

In Bach's organ music two "royal" lines, musical art and
musical science, converge. The organ, representing the scientific
side, had its origin in days of antiquity. It is first mentioned in
the Scriptures in Genesis 4:21, although Jubal's organ was, evi-
dently, just a simple combination of a few pipes. The rudiments
of the modern organ were introduced in the Greek panpipes. But
for centuries the instrument remained unwieldy, some organs of
the tenth century requiring the service of seventy men to manip-
ulate the bellows. Even into the fifteenth century it was necessary
to use the clenched fist to depress a key. Each succeeding generation of organ builders has contributed toward its development
until the organ of today, in dynamic range and resources, in
majestic grandeur, reigns supreme in the realm of tone.

The organ is especially suited to the religious service. In
country church or imposing cathedral, from funeral dirge to
wedding march, it voices the spiritual emotions of men better
than any other musical instrument.

> "But O, what art can teach,
> What human voice can reach,
>   The sacred organ's praise?
> Notes inspiring holy love,
>   Notes that wing their heavenly ways
> To mend the choirs above."
>   —JOHN DRYDEN.

The organ was the center of Bach's art. A peer among
organists of the time, he composed music for the organ which
remains unsurpassed. Dr. Spitta, noted authority on Bach's life,
in commenting on his ability as a performer on the organ, says,
"Friends and foes alike here bowed to the irresistible force of an
unheard-of power of execution, and could hardly comprehend

how he could twist his fingers and his feet so wonderfully and so nimbly without hitting a single false note or displacing his body with violent swaying."

Similarly, an eyewitness wrote, "With his two feet he could perform on the pedals passages which would be enough to provoke many a skilled clavier player with five fingers." Some conception of his large physique may be gained from the size of his left hand, which was capable of spanning twelve keys.

In his position as chapelmaster at Cothen, offered to him by Prince Leopold, the composer and his new patron became inseparable companions, making numerous trips together. While returning from one of these excursions, Bach was shocked to learn that his wife had died while he was away. This left him with the sole care of four of his seven children. Three had preceded the mother in death.

The following year Bach was married to Anna Magdalena Wulken, and the broken home was re-established. A happy home it proved to be for a period of almost thirty years, until the death of the father in 1750. Children came to bless that home —thirteen more. These, together with the four from Bach's first marriage, made the family large enough to form its own orchestra or choral society. Several of the sons showed exceptional musical talent, although not in any way comparable with that of the father.

The Bachs subscribed to the prevailing custom among musicians of maintaining one or more music notebooks. These scrapbooks of favorite pieces were kept with fastidious care, and became a particular source of family pride. Father Sebastian began filling several of these notebooks shortly after his marriage, one of the early compositions being a bridal song. He had one album elaborately bound and inscribed to his wife, "Anna Magdalena Bachin." Most of the compositions are religious in style; a few are secular and in reflective mood. Although a number of Bach's manuscripts were lost, several of his family notebooks have come down to us. One of these has been acquired by the Yale Music Library at a cost of $40,000.

Leipzig, center of learning, next beckoned for the services of the master. Beginning as cantor of the St. Thomas school for boys, Bach spent the last twenty-seven years of his life there. The duties of the cantor included teaching singing and Latin, as well as certain duties as preceptor, together with the super-vision of the music for Sundays and holydays. Lack of apprecia-tion of music was common not only on the part of the boys but also on the part of some of the rectors. Disputes and problems arose to harass the not-always-serene cantor. Occasionally a wig, together with caustic words, would fly in the direction of some unfortunate scholar showing demerit in an assignment either from lack of talent or from lack of preparation.

Nevertheless, routine duties were not allowed to interfere with his calling as a composer, for Bach did a large part of his composition along choral lines while at Leipzig. Chorals, can-tatas, and the Passion music were written in order to furnish appropriate music for the Sunday and holyday services through-out the year. These reflected his conviction that "the object of all music should be the glory of God." The following lines from one of his chorals represent his fundamental convictions:

> "Before Thy throne, my God, I stand;
> Myself, my all, are in Thy hand.
> Turn to me Thine approving face,
> Nor from me now withhold Thy grace.

> "Grant Thou my end may worthy be
> And that I wake Thy face to see,
> Thyself forevermore to know.
> Amen, amen, God grant it so!"

A deep sense of piety is evident not only in the sacred music of Bach but in his secular works as well. The master inscribed many of his scores with "Jesus, help" at the beginning, and "To God alone the glory" at the close. Bach combined in his sacred compositions the highest and purest musical expression with the deepest and most touching feelings of devotion. He offered his musical gifts as incense to the Giver.

Bach spent his entire life in Germany, and although he was
acquainted with the styles of other composers and schools, his
work remains Teutonic, uninfluenced by the popular tastes of
the day. He was content to live, quietly and obscurely, for his
family, his art, and his God. His modest nature was evidenced
when he replied to one who praised his skill at the organ.
"There is nothing very wonderful about it. You have only to
strike the right key at the right time, and the instrument does
the rest." In similar vein he said on another occasion, "Anyone
could do as much as I have done if he worked as hard."

The composer, as was true of his contemporaries Handel and
Milton, became blind in his later years. But the vision of his
soul remained undimmed, and the fertile creations of his genius
continued until his death at the age of sixty-five years.

Bach's service to music transcends that of any other man
in the history of the art. He was the champion of the tempered
scale, in which the tonal scale was tuned so that there were
twelve equal half steps to the octave. This is the basis for our
present system of transition and modulation.

The conventional fingering of Bach's day used the three
middle fingers of either hand, placing them in a prone position
on the keys. He raised the hand and wrist, and made use of all the
fingers, including the thumbs.

Bach's music is the culmination of the polyphonic style,
which required not only a vertical attitude as in our present-day
harmonic system, but a horizontal attitude, as well, as is true
especially in the fugues, where themes or melodies, generally
short, are given to one voice and then to another, resulting in an
almost constant interweaving of independent parts.

Then, like a musical prophet, Bach anticipated the forms and
styles that were further developed by masters, such as Haydn,
Mozart, Beethoven, and others. Although written for the clavichord and harpsichord, predecessors of the piano, his music—
especially the *Well-tempered Clavichord,* forty-eight preludes
and fugues in twenty-four different keys—is an indispensable
part of the present-day pianist's repertoire. "If all music were to

perish and this one opus were saved, it would serve as the key-stone of a new era of musical development."

In the English and French suites, as well as the *partitas* of Bach, a musical form that had been in vogue since the latter part of the sixteenth century, reached its culmination. Basically the suite consisted of four dance movements, generally in iden-tical keys. The cycle of movements began with the *allemande* and was followed by the courante, which was chosen from either the French or the Italian types. The third movement, the saraband, was slow and dignified in style. It occupied a central position in the suite, like the keystone of a musical arch. The *gigue*, gay and rollicking, concluded the cycle. Various other dances, such as a gavotte, a *bourree*, or a minuet, were often introduced between the saraband and the *gigue*.

Bach's instrumental compositions include also the two- and three-part inventions, the *Goldberg Variations*, the *Italian Concerto*, and other concertos for the piano; fugues, variations, or-gan chorales, and chorale preludes for the organ; violin and cello sonatas; orchestral suites and six Brandenburg concertos; *The Musical Offering*, based on a theme by Frederick the Great; and *The Art of the Fugue*, evaluated by musicologists as the greatest of all contrapuntal works of musical history.

The pre-eminence of Bach's mastery and the matchless treasures of his genius were forgotten for a century after his passing. True, there had been instances when the clear light of his greatness dawned on minds open to musical truth. When Mozart visited the Thomasschule at Leipzig, in 1789, he heard for the first time Bach's motet "Sing Unto the Lord a New Song," performed by the choir.

"Mozart knew this master more by hearsay than by his works," wrote an eyewitness, F. Rochlitz. He continues, "Hardly had the choir sung a few measures when Mozart sat up, startled; a few measures more and he called out: 'What is this?' And now his whole soul seemed to be in his ears. When the singing was finished he cried out, full of joy: 'Now, there is something one can learn from!' He was told that this school, in which

Sebastian Bach had been cantor, possessed the complete collection of his motets and preserved them as a sort of sacred relic. 'That's the spirit! That's fine!' he cried. 'Let's see them!' There was, however, no score of these songs, so he had the parts given to him; and then it was for the silent observer a joy to see how eagerly Mozart sat himself down, with the parts all around him—in both hands, on his knees, and on the chairs next to him—and, forgetting everything else, did not get up again until he looked through everything of Sebastian Bach's that was there."

But it was Mendelssohn, then a zealous youth of twenty, who, through his revival of the *St. Matthew Passion,* gave impetus to a rediscovery of Bach's masterpieces. The enthusiastic reception accorded the first performance of this choral work in 1829 led to other performances and to a revival of the *B minor Mass,* and the *St. John Passion.* These in turn led to the oratorios and cantatas.

The genius of Bach, one of the supreme music masters, issued from the union of a complete mastery of musical art with the strength of character necessary to its diligent pursuit. The editors of *The Bach Reader* attribute the power of his music to "its monumental proportions, its contrapuntal intensity, its rhythmic consistency, . . . to the cogency of his themes, the expressiveness of his melodies, the force and richness of his harmony, the diversity and logic of his orchestration." Music of such excellence and character was dependent for its complete fulfillment on the character of its creator. In integrity, in resourcefulness, in attention to duty, Bach the *man* fulfilled the demands of Bach the *musician.*

In accord with the practice of appropriating the names of objects of nature as family surnames, as used in certain European countries, the name Bach signifies a "brook." Even so, Bach's work, beginning as a small stream in the wooded hills of old Thuringia, has gained velocity and volume while passing down the "mountains" of the years, until today, in musical worth and depth of emotional expression, its scope is like the mighty ocean.

George Frideric Handel

George Frideric Handel

1685-1759

"I did not intend to amuse or afford pleasure; I meant to make the world better."

HERE were giants in the earth in those days." This Scriptural reference to the antediluvians could easily have its counterpart in the lives of two men born in the latter part of the seventeenth century. Musical giants, to be sure; their service to religion and music is nothing short of herculean.

Handel and Bach were both born in 1685, just one month apart, in adjoining provinces of Germany. Their parallel lives, now similar, now opposite, are reflected in the styles adopted in their musical creations.

Handel had no musical ancestry, whereas Bach had that of centuries. Both were great organists and harpsichordists. Both were of large physique. Both were Lutherans. Both became blind. Handel was a bachelor, but Bach was twice married. Handel, a man of the world, showed in his works the influence of the Italian and English tastes; Bach, self-confined throughout his life to certain parts of his native country, remained unaffected in his individual style by the voice of the multitude. The art of Handel is the more practical by reason of its universal melodic and dramatic appeal. On the other hand, that of Bach is the more

2

profound in its artistic perfection and depth of emotional expression.

The father of George Frideric Handel was a surgeon-barber, ambitious, able, and practical; the mother, thirty years younger, was known for her pious and charitable deeds. In Halle, Saxony, where Papa Handel had established a comfortable home, George Frideric was born, the second of four children of his father's second marriage.

Early in his boyhood George, charmed by the world of sound and the lure of melody, took the keenest delight in playing with horns, drums, and other musical toys. Papa Handel looked on with an amused twinkle in his eye until he began to realize that the thumping and blowing were becoming more than a mere pastime with George, and for the son of a respectable surgeon-barber to become a musician was out of the question. Thereafter the toys were taken from him and everything possible was done to discourage the musical inclinations of the boy.

The father's disparaging attitude toward music and musicians should not be judged too harshly in view of the place then held by musicians in the social and economic scale. Some were underpaid as church musicians; others were reduced to mere vassals in a royal household; and a great many more were but common street musicians, going from door to door to eke out an existence. Such a means of livelihood could not be sanctioned by so practical a man as Father Handel. But genius knows no shackles.

In some manner the child not only managed to hear music but learned to play the clavichord as well, so that before he was ten years old he surprised his listeners by his ability. Nevertheless, the father remained adamant in his decision; his son would study law.

One day the elder Handel and George, then eight or nine years old, boarded a carriage to visit a relative employed on the estate of the Duke of Saxe-Weissenfels. The twenty-five-mile trip began as an innocent pleasure jaunt. But, contrary to the father's plans, it was to mark the first stage of a long and adventurous journey for George.

Soon after they arrived at the estate, the child's curiosity about things on the grounds led him to the chapel—and to the organ. The presiding organist, seeing the keen interest shown by the lad, lifted him onto the bench, whereupon George, half sitting and half standing, delightedly explored the huge tone box. Here was no toy. Cautiously, at first, he tried the various stops: principal, gamba, and on through the entire registration. Then, with rising confidence, he proceeded to combine the tonal colors into harmonic and polyphonic designs until the power of the *full* organ thrilled his little soul.

The duke overheard the music, and upon inquiry, learned the identity of the prodigy. He immediately summoned the elder Handel and his son, and urged the father to encourage the development of the superior talent shown by the boy. After much persuasion the father consented to place George with a music teacher upon return to their native city. George was happy; he was now free to revel in sweet sounds and to make real his childish musical fancies.

For a number of years thereafter George Frideric studied various branches of music, including organ, violin, and composition, with Friedrich Zachau, a Halle musician, and a feeling of mutual admiration and respect grew up between teacher and pupil. How often when the sunlight of success shines upon the great men and women of history, there is cast, in the preparatory background of their lives, a dual shadow—their own and that of a parent, a teacher, or a friend who has been willing to sacrifice his own ambitions in order to develop the talents of those placed in his charge. Handel, throughout his career, cherished the memory of his first teacher.

As a youth of eighteen George Frideric left his home and settled for a time in Hamburg. Here a friendship was formed with Johann Mattheson, a talented musician and versatile gentleman, four years older than Handel.

In a search for a remunerative position as a church organist, Handel learned that the aging Buxtehude, organist at Lubeck, was looking for a successor. So Handel and Mattheson, as friendly rivals, set out for Lubeck. Like two gallant princes aspiring to the throne of a retiring musical monarch, their spirits ran high, until, in the presence of the king, they were reminded that, according to custom, he who inherits the kingdom, takes, moreover, the hand of the crown princess. The young men had already met the elderly, unattractive daughter of Buxtehude. The glory of the kingdom faded.

Across the Alps into Italy, Handel wandered; to bask in the sunshine of its passionate music, to imbibe the nectar of its graceful melody, and to feel the pulse of its dramatic temperament. His three-year sojourn in Florence, Naples, and other Italian cities served as an important background for his future work, especially in the operatic field. As a composer and harpsichordist, Handel won an enviable place in the hearts of the Italian people during his stay there.

Even as Handel was sojourning in and about Florence, where one of his earliest operas was performed in 1707, a real-life music drama was being enacted in the hills overlooking the city. The Grand Duke of Tuscany, whom Handel visited, had in his employ a prominent harpsichord maker, Bartolommeo Cristofori. Early in the eighteenth century Cristofori's workshop was the scene of numerous experiments as the inventor sought to substitute a hammer action for the quill-plucking action of the harpsichord. The revolutionary idea of the hammer action had had the attention of earlier inventors, but to Cristofori's instrument, which he brought out about 1711, is conceded the historical prerogative of being the earliest piano.

Although the Cristofori pianoforte was a fragile instrument compared with the pianos of the present day, it was the genesis of a succession of developments that culminated in the versatile instrument of our time. The piano has been designated as a "veritable microcosm of music," with a mechanism so delicately adjusted that a finger pressure of two and one-half ounces on a key is sufficient to produce a *pianissimo* tone, and with a frame so sturdily constructed as to support a combined string tension of twenty tons.

The invention of the piano marked the beginning of a new musical era. Handel was not to concern himself with the new instrument, but, together with Bach, Scarlatti of Italy, and Rameau of France, would bring the harpsichord era to a glorious climax. To hear a Handel suite, Bach's *Italian Concerto,* or a Scarlatti sonata on the harpsichord is to hear them ideally. Its crisp, discreet, and stringy tone quality seems to evoke the spirit and times of the masters of the seventeenth and eighteenth centuries, even to the days when the youthful Handel awed the people of Florence and Venice with his harpsichord virtuosity.

The young musician left the land of song and returned to Germany to become the chapelmaster to the elector of Hanover. Shortly afterward, on leave, he set out for England by way of Holland, first visiting his mother and his former teacher, Zachau, at Halle. To his relatives and to those who had befriended him in his childhood, Handel ever showed the most tender devotion.

By this time Handel's reputation as a composer had spread to other countries, including England. Hence, on his arrival in London, in 1710, he was immediately taken into the heart of the English people. He, in turn, took the English people into his great heart. He entered into his new environment with zest, and erelong composed the opera *Rinaldo,* which was produced in the great metropolis with considerable success.

An interesting personality who lived in London at this time was Thomas Britton. He earned a livelihood by peddling coal carried in a sack on his back. After walking the streets of the city during the day, he repaired in the evening to his two-story stable house, washed himself, changed his garments, and made ready to entertain the musical elite of the city who came to his humble, meagerly furnished house to participate in the intellectual discussions and to hear the finest chamber music. "Poor, lowborn, and entirely self-educated, this humble amateur was one of nature's truest gentlemen." Handel was among the regular visitors to the "coal man's" musicales, and it was here that he became acquainted with many men of letters and art lovers of the city.

The six months Handel spent in London passed only too quickly. He returned to Hanover to resume his duties at the court, composed some chamber music, and studied diligently to perfect his art. But his heart was in England. He obtained a second leave of absence, on condition that he would return within a reasonable time, and left for another visit to England in 1712. Obviously the Saxon musicïan changed his mind with regard to the length of his leave, for he continued to live in England the remainder of his life, with the exception of visits to his native country and to Italy.

Queen Anne of England, who had appointed Handel as composer to the British court, died in 1714. George I, the elector of Hanover, with whom the composer had been associated in Germany, succeeded her on the throne. Thus, suddenly, Handel was deprived of his allotted pension and, furthermore, he was now held in disfavor by the new king in that he had not returned to his position as chapelmaster at Hanover.

That Handel was able to reinstate himself in the good graces of the king is evident in Handel's role in a royal water party in 1717. On an evening of mid-July the nobility, headed by the king, sailed up the Thames River, escorted by craft of various styles and sizes. As seen from the shore, the flotilla gave the appearance of a huge water carnival. The boats were illuminated by means of lanterns hung on the riggings. In the wake of the royal barge, Handel, with an orchestra of fifty members under his direction, followed in another boat. For the occasion the composer had written sarabands, hornpipes, and other dance movements. Throughout the entire evening his now famous *Water Music* furnished entertainment for the royal party as they proceeded between Whitehall and Limehouse. The king was so pleased with the splendor of the music and ingenuity of its aquatic setting that he commanded that the music be played three times during the course of the evening.

The composer became a naturalized British subject in 1726. Thereafter, his corpulent figure, in "gold-laced coat, ruffles, cocked hat, and sword," was a familiar sight in the theaters, churches, and on the streets of the English capital. In personal appearance and temperament Handel resembled Dr. Samuel Johnson. Their similarities are aptly stated by one author when he says: "Both had booming voices, gruff manners, testy tempers, Gargantuan appetites, a dynamic gusto for living, an overflowing reservoir of energy, and kindly hearts tucked away under more or less forbidding exteriors; both knew practically everybody worth knowing in London—a London that was bubbling over with wit, talent, and genius."

For nearly four decades there was to issue from Handel's residence at 57 Brook Street an almost incessant flow of music, including some of the most sublime choral pieces ever written. It would encompass the best of his forty operas and many of his instrumental creations. The members of his household would witness the wearisome activities that make up the life of an impresario. They would observe firsthand a German composer successfully producing Italian operas in an English capital. They would speak of his simple home life. They would know of his keen appreciation for the paintings of the masters. They would vouch for his integrity, smile at his wit, defer to his independence, boast of his generosity.

A set of suites for harpsichord, published in 1720, launched Handel's ventures in the field of instrumental composition. The fifth of this set, the *Suite in E major,* contains the storied "Harmonious Blacksmith" variations. The composer's other instrumental works include twelve *Concerti grossi,* six concertos for organ and orchestra, violin sonatas, oboe concertos, and the *Royal Fireworks Music,* written for an outdoor festival occasion celebrating the Peace of Aix-la-Chapelle.

Fortunately for the world, and for religion and the musical art in particular, Handel, at the age of fifty-three, left the operatic field and turned his wholehearted attention to the oratorio. His rare gifts, mature experience, and religious background eminently fitted him to present the Biblical stories in masterly musical settings. A few of the oratorios from his facile pen are *Saul, Israel in Egypt, Judas Maccabaeus, Samson,* and *The Messiah.*

By the time Handel had reached the age of fifty-six he had run the gamut of human experience. He could look back over pleasant days of affluence, of public favor, of honorable position, and of prodigious creative accomplishments. But now reverses set in and met him at every step. Poverty, jealousies by his professional and political rivals, loss of public patronage, and declining health contributed to try his spirit.

But he rose above all difficulties, rallied his strength and resources, and in the short period of twenty-four days, with little food or sleep, wrote the monumental masterpiece—*The Messiah*. When he reached the "Hallelujah Chorus," "among all Hallelujahs in music, the alpha and omega, the only one!" Handel wrote afterward, "I did think I did see all heaven before me and the great God Himself."

Despite his own impoverishment, Handel was ever willing to assist those who were in want. Accordingly, when an invitation was extended by the viceroy of Ireland for the composer to present his own music in Dublin at a charitable benefit, Handel immediately accepted. He sailed for Dublin soon after with the *Messiah* manuscript included in his luggage. Alexander Pope commemorated the episode when he wrote:

> "But soon, ah soon, rebellion will commence,
> If music meanly borrows aid from sense.
> Strong in new arms, lo! Giant Handel stands,
> Like bold Briareus, with a hundred hands;
> To stir, to rouse, to shake the soul he comes,
> And Jove's own thunders follow Mars's Drums,
> Arrest him, empress; or you sleep no more—
> She heard, and drove him to the Hibernian shore."

A Dublin newspaper advertisement appeared in the latter part of March, 1742, announcing the forthcoming concert of Handel's *Messiah* to take place on April 12, 1742. It was requested that the ladies appear without hoops and the gentlemen without swords. As a result of this ban on accessories and accouterments, space was made available to accommodate about a hundred more persons in the hall. About two thousand dollars was raised for charitable purposes.

It is now a little over two hundred years since the auspicious *premiere* of *The Messiah*. Through the centuries countless thousands have had their hearts renewed and their faith strengthened in the promises of the Redeemer through the medium of the sublime musical setting of these promises in this grand oratorio.

The impression of one musical disciple, on hearing the oratorio, illustrates its sublime effectiveness. "We feel," he wrote, "on returning from hearing *The Messiah,* as if we had shaken off some of our dirt and dross, as if the world were not so much with us; our hearts are elevated, and yet subdued, as if the glow of some action, or the grace of some noble principle had passed over us. We are conscious of having indulged in an enthusiasm which cannot lead us astray, of tasting a pleasure which is not of the forbidden tree, for it is the only one which is distinctly promised to be translated with us from earth to heaven."

The Messiah may properly be regarded as the "sun" of Handel's achievements. So bright has been its light, so impressive has been its scope and stature, that it has eclipsed much of the remaining library of Handelian scores. What hidden treasures lie buried in these forgotten masterpieces! It stirs the imagination to wish to explore the harvest of more than a half century of unremitting creative activity. The composer's church music, taken alone, included more than twenty-five oratorios, and a dozen anthems. Those who know Handel best are scanning the horizon for signs of a renaissance of his master works. "When that rediscovery takes place," comments Herbert Weinstock in his book *Handel*, "his whole voice will break on the musical world at once familiar and new, one of the most majestic, tender, and human voices ever lifted in praise of life, of love, of beauty, and of the art of music."

Shortly after he returned to London, Handel's *Samson* was presented at Covent Garden. The text of this oratorio is taken largely from Milton's "Samson Agonistes," which in turn is based on the Scriptural story of Samson. The work became immediately popular. Handel's prestige was returning. New creations, new friends, new triumphs. And then—darkness. Loss of his sight began overtaking him while he was engaged in the composition of *Jeptha's Daughter*. After a few months he became totally blind.

On an evening in the spring of 1759 the oratorio *Samson* was again given in Covent Garden, London. A rapt audience listened quietly, reverently. The composer sat near the organ. The music had reached the aria of *Samson* in which the Israelite touchingly laments his blindness:

> "Total clipse, no sun, no moon
> All dark amidst the blaze of noon."

Handel silently wept. The sum total of his human experience was filled. He alone understood.

On April 14, 1759, Handel died. A personal friend, John Smyth, wrote: "He died as he lived, a good Christian, with a true sense of his duty to God and man, and in perfect charity to all the world." He was buried in the Poet's Corner of Westminster Abbey.

> "The silent organ loudest chants
> The Master's requiem."

Franz Joseph Haydn

1732-1809

*"At the thought of God, my heart leaps for joy,
and I cannot help my music's doing the same."*

*I*T IS springtime in Lower Austria—1732. All the countryside pulsates with new life as the fetters of winter are broken. In streams, in groves, and on the mountain slopes is seen the sudden, rushing transformation of nature. From every hamlet and village resound the happy voices of carefree children.

On the banks of the Leitha River, a short distance from Vienna, the little market town of Rohrau is situated. In one of its little peasant cottages lives a master wheelwright, Matthias Haydn, with his small family.

There is considerable excitement in the humble hut this morning, for Frau Haydn gave birth to a son—her second—shortly after midnight. All morning neighboring peasant women have been calling to see the new arrival. At times their conversation becomes rather animated as one insists that the little fellow resembles his father, while another sees the features of his mother, and a third sees no resemblance whatever. As the babble subsides there is heard the wailing obbligato of the new-born babe.

27

Franz Joseph Haydn

The boy is christened Franz Joseph. His mother confides to her husband that she has cherished a secret longing that someday Joseph will take the orders of the church and become a priest. As God-fearing parents, they strive to instill into the hearts of their children not only love for God and the church but love for order, neatness, honesty, and industry as well.

Joseph is nearly five now. As this is Sunday afternoon, his father plays over some of the simple songs that he knows, and little Joseph sings them with his soft, sweet voice. After a little while Joseph finds two pieces of wood, places one over his left shoulder and with the other scrapes back and forth over it in imitation of the violinists he has heard. His father is quite pleased—Joseph's love and aptitude for music are growing.

Months pass. The Haydns are having guests. Among the visitors is a distant relative, Johann Frankh, a schoolmaster from the neighboring market town of Hainburg. In the course of the afternoon Joseph sings for the esteemed guest, who is delighted with the voice and talent of the boy, and suggests that Joseph return with him to Hainburg and receive training in the Catholic choir of that town. The suggestion appeals to the parents as a wise plan, not only on Joseph's behalf, but also on behalf of the growing family, whose burdens may be thereby lessened.

So at six Joseph learns of the ways of the world—far from the tender care of his father and mother, the prattle of his younger brothers and sisters, and the affection and warmth of home. He learns to play the violin and the piano. He sings in the choir. Sometimes his love of fun gets the better of him as he snips off a pigtail from the wig of a choir member in front of him; and then he is given a sound thrashing by the schoolmaster. But worse than a thrashing is an empty stomach and poor Joseph is learning what hunger really means, for the schoolmaster's wife, at whose table Joseph boards, is indifferent to the needs of a growing boy and allows him but scanty fare. It is only his naturally brave spirit and his love for good music that keep him from returning home.

The time for the Week of the Cross Festival has arrived—

May 11-18. Peasants are gathering from the towns and country-side to take part in the annual jubilee. What a colorful appear-ance these Austrian peasants make in their native costumes. But alas! the drummer is ill and cannot take part in the pro-cession. And what is a band without a drummer? The school-master comes to the rescue; he explains the situation to his protege, Joseph. Together they improvise a drum and drumsticks, the former made from a cloth stretched tightly over a basket of meal and placed on an overstuffed chair. Joseph drums away furiously until the meal flies out and covers the room.

Here comes the band! The air is filled with hilarity, patriotic fervor, merry tunes, martial rhythms, gay costumes, and shouts of glee. Before the onlookers passes a comical figure: a large boy with a drum on his back, followed by little Joseph, oblivious to the jests of the spectators, and beating the drum with gusto and precision. No one in the whole festival enjoys himself more than the little drummer.

Festivals, too, must come to a close. Days after, it is rumored that a Viennese musician is in town. He is the court chapelmaster and music director at the cathedral in Vienna. In his search of talent for the St. Stephen's boy choir, his attention is called to Joseph's musical precocity by Schoolmaster Frankh. The visit-ing musician becomes keenly interested in the pleasing voice and the sight-reading ability of the boy. And so, before long, happy Joseph is packing his few personal belongings and is on his way to Vienna to become a member of the boy choir in the cathedral.

There the boys of the choir live together in a house near the cathedral. In addition to instruction in singing and instrumental music they are taught writing, arithmetic, Latin, and theology. During his spare time Joseph cannot resist the urge to place notes on paper; the blacker the finished page looks, the better he likes it. The boys are given a meager allowance, and their food and clothing are anything but the best. Nevertheless, because the boys are young and healthy, they remain fun-loving and mis-chievous, and in mischief-making Joseph is still a ringleader.

As Joseph grows older his changing voice makes his singing

no longer suitable as a boy soprano. The director is looking for an excuse to dismiss the lad from the choir, and so when Joseph again gets into mischief during a choir rehearsal, the director seizes this pretext, canes the boy, and turns him out on the streets of Vienna, at seventeen, a homeless waif.

Like a gypsy, he wanders the streets of the city, hungry, without money, and with few friends. He thinks of returning home, but he knows his parents are already overburdened with a large family. He sees no alternative but to stay on in Vienna.

As the darkness of a November night covers the city and the street lamps are being lit, Joseph, chilled to the bone, still roams the streets with no prospects of either supper or a place to lodge. Hours afterward, his friend Spangler, a chorister, finds him almost exhausted, and takes the lad home to his little attic room to share it with him.

A small sum of money, borrowed from another Viennese friend, enables Joseph to rent a little garret room in the old *Michaelerhaus*. There is neither stove nor window; the roof leaks when it rains or snows; a "worm-eaten clavier" stands in one corner of the room. From these humble surroundings Joseph leaves each day to earn a scanty subsistence by giving a few music lessons, by tuning claviers, and by playing at balls in the winter evenings or on the street corners on the warm evenings of summer. At night he diligently studies the sonatas of P. E. Bach and the works of other composers; he also composes works of his own, including his first mass.

It so happens that one of Haydn's pupils is also a pupil of the noted Italian singing teacher, Porpora. Haydn plays the accompaniments for this pupil and in this way becomes acquainted with the singing master. As the latter is also a thorough teacher in composition, Haydn determines to study composition and Italian with him.

In lieu of money he places his personal services at the disposal of Porpora. He brushes his clothes, shines his shoes, and does a number of menial tasks for lessons. When the old teacher leaves for Mannersdorf, Haydn accompanies him, and there they meet a number of musicians, notably Gluck, the opera composer.

Haydn now finds employment in the service of Baron von Furnberg, and while here his developing talents find expression in the composition of string quartets, trios, and works for wind instruments. Erelong an offer of a position from a Bohemian nobleman, Count Morzin, is accepted. A small private orchestra, at the count's country house near Pilsen, placed under his direction, affords him opportunity for experiments in orchestral coloring and for testing his ensemble writing.

Alongside his regular duties the composer finds time to give some private lessons. Among his pupils are the two daughters of a wigmaker. Joseph loves the younger. However, when he proposes to her after a short courtship, he learns that she is to enter a convent. So the young musician—disillusioned—learns anew that in the symphony of life the tempo is more often grave than lively, and the somber melodic strains outnumber the gay.

The girl's father, wishing to have Haydn marry into his family, suggests that he marry his older daughter. Strangely enough, although she is unattractive and three years older than the composer, he begins courting her, and their wedding is announced for November 26, 1760.

Too late Haydn learns that his bride is "heartless, unsociable, quarrelsome, extravagant, and bigoted." She cares not whether he is "an artist or a cobbler." She uses his compositions for curling paper. Not even his own genial nature can quiet the perpetual marital tempests. Possibly as an outlet for his pent-up feelings he composes a canon on a poem by Lessing:

"If in the whole wide world
But one mean wife there is,
How sad that each of us
Should think this one is his!"

Meanwhile, the young musician is advanced to a position in the service of Prince Esterhazy. The written contract specifies that the composer is to "know his place, to be quiet, sober, and modest toward his superiors, to be always in uniform, to compose all the necessary music for His Highness's entertainment, to write nothing for anyone else without His .Highness's permission, to obey with the greatest exactitude all the orders he may receive from His Highness, and to take his meals with the other domestics." How does the composer feel about his position as a servant? He replies, "It is indeed sad to be a slave but Providence wills it, and so I must bear it."

Albeit, his position is not without compensating advantages. His salary is ample. The surroundings of the palace are delightful, with "a deer park, flower gardens, and hothouses, elaborately furnished summerhouses, grottoes, hermitages, and temples." Several well-equipped theaters for operatic and orchestral concerts adorn the grounds. To the members of the orchestra and the band of singers under his direction the composer is affectionately known as "Papa Haydn," indicating that his associations are pleasant.

For diversion Haydn is fond of hunting, fishing, and especially traveling. But the prince is generally reluctant to give a vacation to his musicians, because he wishes to have them on the palace grounds at all times for any need that may arise.

The season is late. Prince Esterhazy has arranged for a holiday concert. For the occasion the composer has written his *Farewell Symphony*. The concert is already well in progress. As the finale of the *Farewell Symphony* is reached and as the theme develops, a member of the orchestra arises, blows out his candle, and leaves the room. Now another member does likewise, and another, until only Haydn, who is directing, remains, head bowed, near his desk. Even the prince enjoys the suggestive jest. "If all go," says he "we may as well go, too."

After a most enjoyable vacation at Vienna, Haydn is again with Esterhazy. He sits at his writing desk, reminiscing over the pleasant days at the Viennese capital. To a friend he writes: "Here I am again in solitude—abandoned—like a poor orphan —almost without human companionship—sad—filled with the memory of happy days gone by. . . . And who knows when these pleasant days will return? That happy company, a whole circle of friends united in heart and soul, all those delightful musical evenings, . . . where are they now? They are past, and it will be long before they come again."

But before long the monotony of his daily duties is forgotten in the joy of creative achievements. His love of fun, so marked in his younger days, stays with him during his advancing years. Everywhere in his music his effervescent humor manifests itself. A well-known example is found in the *Surprise Symphony* in which, in the midst of a tranquil passage, a sudden fortissimo chord rends the air—like a clap of thunder from a cloudless sky. "This will make the ladies jump!" chuckles the composer.

Haydn is a pioneer in the field of the string quartet, that charmingly intimate ensemble of bowed instruments. "His quartets," writes Nathan Dole, "have been compared to the conversations of four amiable and intellectual persons: the first violin, a middle-aged man of wit and good humor, a good talker, taking rather more than his share of the conversation; the second violin, a friend of the first, rarely occupied with himself, intent on repeating and seconding the ideas broached by the first; the bass, learned and sententious, with laconic but set opinions, sometimes prophetic like one versed in the affairs of the world; while the viola is a bright-tempered matron, not apt to indulge in very deep or important remarks, but adding a touch of grace to the whole."

In the purely classical school, of which Haydn is a vital link, emphasis is placed in the logical and formal presentation of musical ideas. The musical seed thoughts grow into sentences, then paragraphs, and finally into large movements. The resulting musical forms—sonatina, rondo, sonata, and variation—were the designs generally chosen to express the classical style. A verse by H. C. Bunner illustrates the design of the rondo form:

> "A pitcher of mignonette
>   In a tenement's highest casement,
>   Queer sort of flower-pot—yet
>   That pitcher of mignonette

Is a garden in heaven set,
　To the little sick child in the basement—
The pitcher of mignonette,
　In the tenement's highest casement."

The sonata is the highest harmonic form of instrumental classical music. It is the ideal medium for expressing music in a balanced and symmetrical style. Haydn's contribution toward the development and perfection of this form is sufficient in itself to reserve for him a niche in music's hall of fame. This design is used for solo instruments, string quartets, trios, symphonies, and concertos. There are generally four movements: the first, usually in sonata form; the second, a slow movement; the third, a dance form, such as a minuet and trio, or a scherzo and trio; and the fourth, the finale.

Briefly, the sonata form proper has three main divisions with the first division, or exposition, consisting of two contrasting themes, the first masculine, rhythmic, dynamic, and incisive, while the second is feminine, persuasive, and lyric, and is in a neighboring key. In the second division, or development, the two themes appear in disguise, masquerading, as it were, in costumes of altered rhythms, varying moods, and changing melodic curves. In the third division, or return, the two original themes occur in the same "home" key. A coda closes the movement.

As the fame of Haydn's work spreads to other countries, he is invited to visit Italy and England. Finally he accepts. All arrangements have been made, and he is about to make his first visit to London in December, 1790. Before Haydn leaves Vienna, the young Mozart, to whom he has become affectionately attached, tries to dissuade him: "Oh, Papa, you have no training for the wide, wide world, and you speak too few languages." "My language," replies Haydn, "is understood the world over."

So to London he journeys. There a royal welcome awaits him, and he is feted and revered by small and great alike. When it becomes necessary for him to return to Vienna, wealth and fame attend him. His second visit to London several years later

is even more successful. At this visit his long-cherished desire to
write an oratorio is given a decided impetus by his hearing a
performance of Handel's *Messiah* at Westminster Abbey.

On his return to Hungary, Haydn although sixty-six years of
age, begins work on the oratorio *Creation,* basing it on the
Genesis story and on Milton's *Paradise Lost.* Two years are spent
on its composition. "I spend much time on it," says the master,
"because I intend it to last a long time." With the work completed
he writes: "Never was I so pious as when I engaged upon the
Creation. I fell on my knees daily and prayed earnestly to God
that He would grant me strength to carry out the work, and to
praise Him worthily."

In his sixty-eighth year Haydn is urgently requested by his
friends to write another oratorio. But as is common with many
composers, who, late in life, are fearful lest their creative powers
are waning, he answers, "I am afraid that the oil in the cruse
will not hold out." But it does hold out, and *The Seasons* comes
forth as his last great masterpiece. When asked his opinion of the
comparative musical worth of *The Creation* and *The Seasons,*
he replies, "I esteem *The Creation* higher, for in it the angels of
God appear but in *The Seasons* it is only the peasant, Simon,
that talks." *The Creation* extols the Creator while *The Seasons*
describes, musically, the beauties of nature.

It is March 27, 1808. Haydn is now seventy-six. Despite
his advanced age and frailty he is to attend a performance of
The Creation in a music hall at Vienna this evening. Important
personages in government and musical circles are already in their
seats. From his carriage Haydn is carried into the auditorium
in an armchair. As he is borne in, blasts of trumpets and shouts
of "Long live Haydn" greet him. At the passage, "And there
was light," the audience breaks into thunderous applause whereupon the composer lifts his hand toward heaven and exclaims,
"It came from thence!"

The curtain on Haydn's life is slowly lowering. His devoted
servants are doing everything possible to make his last days
comfortable. Today he asks that he be carried to his clavier.

Three times he gravely plays the "Emperor's Hymn"—his parting hymn to music. A few days later, with the assurance "that I have done my duty," as he had earlier expressed it, he passes into the valley of the shadow.

The story of Haydn's life is a story wherein the stony ground of forbidding circumstances was made to yield fruits of achievement, both rich and abundant. He had come up from poverty and misfortune. Reflecting on his early days, he once said, "Young people can learn from my example that something can come out of nothing. What I am is all the result of the direst need." He made the most of his opportunities and surmounted his difficulties until better fortune came his way. Having been poor, he could dispense his acquired wealth with good judgment. Having been a servant, he knew how to be a gracious master. Having seen the pageantry and pomp of royalty from the "underside," he could walk with kings and not "lose the common touch."

It is to the mature creations of Haydn's crowning years that the world most frequently turns for inspiration and enlightenment. Just as Haydn's life had undergone many changes, so his music had passed through several stages of development. From his early rococo style, with its emphasis on grace and delicacy, his creations moved toward a balanced classical style. Even in his maturity there was a constant search for new modes of expression, an eagerness to attain new musical heights.

Haydn's music still lives. The enduring qualities of his musical contributions have been summarized by Paul Henry Lang in these words: "Haydn's works occupy a definite position in our musical life, a position that could not be filled by anyone or anything else. Love of life, wholesomeness, clarity, purity of feeling, noble and profound sentiments, inexhaustible humor, and impeccable craftsmanship are the characteristic traits of his art which should be treasured by us in whose art they appear so seldom."

Wolfgang Amadeus Mozart

Wolfgang Amadeus Mozart

1756-1791

His Cup of Spontaneous Genius Overflowed

ഗ

MUSIC portrays life. Music *is* life. Fine music is born in the soul travail of a master; it is cradled in the temple of his heart. It reveals the emotions, the experiences, the aspirations, of great men. It appeals to the highest motives of man; it inspires to nobler living.

Just as there is more than one plane of living, so music reaches more than one level of expression. Some music is perverted life; some music represents the slums of human experience. On the other hand, there is music that breathes a prayer and lifts the heart toward God; angel of good, it dispels the shades of night and illumines life's finer paths. Happy is the musical pilgrim who has discovered the gems of melody that lie at his feet.

The name of Mozart is so naturally identified with fine music that *Mozart* has come to mean "beautiful music," and *beautiful music*, Mozart. He flashed across the musical heavens with meteorlike brilliance, and burned out in the dazzling intensity of his own light. In the history of music there has been no more outstanding instance of pure genius. "He was gifted with an extraordinarily keen sense of beauty, and with the most

39

astounding natural facility in all things artistic which ever was the lot of man."

Wolfgang Amadeus Mozart was a boy wonder. As a mere babe of three, he would drop his toys and run to the clavier whenever his sister, Maria Anna, would practice or was to have her music lesson with Papa Mozart. When the lesson was over, Wolfgang clambered onto the bench, and there he would sit by the hour picking out pleasing intervals.

The children inherited their father's broad forehead, large blue-gray eyes, and soft sandy hair. Maria Anna, five years older than Wolfgang, was also a prodigy. The two little musicians were a constant source of pride and joy to Herr Mozart, and he accepted their genius as a mark of divine favor.

Wolfgang was so delicate in body and so serious, even at a very early age, that his loved ones and friends despaired of his life. His extremely sensitive ear could detect a difference of pitch even to an eighth of a tone, and the sharp blast of a trumpet was so painful to him that it caused him to faint. His love for his near ones was especially tender. He would say, "Next after God comes papa."

At four, Wolfgang played little pieces; at five, he had begun to compose. When he tried writing a concerto, and it was found correctly written but too difficult for anyone to play, he had an answer for their misgivings: "That is why it is called a concerto; people must practice it till they can play it perfectly." And again he dipped the quill a little deeper into the inkwell and wiped the blots with his arm or the palm of his hand.

Leopold Mozart, Wolfgang's father, had left the family trade of bookbinding and settled in the picturesque old city of Salzburg. Here his talents on the violin and in composition had won for him a position as court musician in the service of the archbishop, with a steady, although inadequate, salary. A growing discontent with his position and an increasing sense of the pecuniary possibilities attached to showing his precocious children to the world led him finally to succumb to the temptation of exploiting them.

Herr Mozart's ambitions early took shape. In midwinter, with papa as concert manager, the three boarded the coach for Munich, well supplied with blankets, shawls, and tasty lunches, amid parting admonitions from mamma that the children be careful to avoid drafts, keep their feet dry, and eat good food. The coach lunged forward—their concert tours had begun.

They played before the Elector and at important gatherings in the Bavarian capital. Immediately the magic of their playing made them the pets of society. After several weeks they returned to Salzburg with larger plans developing in the mind of Herr Mozart for future tours.

Many months of preparation followed, and the entire family left Salzburg in September, 1762, with Vienna as their goal. The journey was made partly by coach and partly by boat on the Danube. The children appeared at the royal court in a "command" performance which lasted three hours. From the emperor down through the lesser members of the royal household—all lovers of music—lavish praise was heaped on the heads of the "little magician" and his sister.

When the formal presentation was over, Wolfgang, always his natural self, threw his arms around the empress and kissed her, and then scampered off to play with the royal children. While hurrying across the polished floor, the little guest slipped and went sprawling to the floor. Princess Marie Antoinette helped him to his feet. "You are nice," said the six-year-old Wolfgang, "and when I grow up I will marry you." The amused empress asked him why he favored Marie Antoinette over her sisters, and he replied, "Because she was kind to me, while her sisters stood by and did nothing."

The fond attention given Wolfgang and Maria Anna suddenly stopped when Wolfgang came down with scarlet fever. Even after his recovery, people shunned him for fear of contracting the disease. So from palace to humble home the Mozarts steered their course, reaching Salzburg only after a perilous journey in bitter winter weather.

Papa Mozart, pleased with the ripples made by his "musical

pebbles" near the shore, determined to launch farther out into the ocean of fame and fortune. As the "captain of their destiny" he could already hear the waves of applause; perhaps a "deep-sea catch" would come their way to rescue the dwindling family purse.

Paris! No sooner had the family arrived than papa, in the role of press agent, told the Parisians in no uncertain terms of the "astounding genius" of his two children. The advertisement read in part:

"The little girl, who is in her twelfth year, will play the most difficult compositions of the great masters; the boy, who is not yet seven will . . . instantly name all notes played at a distance, whether singly or in chords, on the clavier, or any other instrument. He will finally, both on the harpsichord and the organ, improvise as long as may be desired and in any key."

During the five-month stay in the French capital, the children were showered with glory and gifts. But as Herr Mozart strove to balance the family budget, he found that the expenses of the trip and those entailed in maintaining a social "front" outweighed the monetary gains. There had been more fame than fortune. So he gathered his brood about him and disclosed his further plans for storming another capital, London, with music.

A gracious reception awaited the "prodigies of nature" at St. James's court. King George III and the queen took a special delight in testing Wolfgang's skill at sight reading. The court musician, J. Christian Bach, son of the great Bach, played duets with the little fellow, and the two became intimate friends. He said of Wolfgang: "Many a court musician knew less at the end of his career than Mozart knew at the beginning."

When Papa Mozart took seriously ill, it was necessary for the children to refrain from playing on any instruments; so Wolfgang took to writing a symphony, his first, at the age of eight. Herein lies the difference between Mozart and many other prodigies who have lived through the years. To perform in a masterly manner, remarkable as that is, is one thing, but to *create* is quite another. In view of Mozart's short life, it is fortunate for the world that he began creative work at such an early age.

Homeward bound! The Mozarts journeyed by way of Holland, where the children played before the ruling prince at The Hague, and later played at Amsterdam, at a concert in which all the instrumental compositions were Wolfgang's own. Paris again, then Switzerland, and in the latter part of 1766, the now worldly-wise family reached Salzburg, after having been away more than three years.

Not only was Father Leopold shrewd in business; he was a fine teacher. He soon arranged that Wolfgang's interrupted studies should be resumed, and laid careful plans for his future career. Even the mighty flow of genius must be harnessed, lest it waste itself in dissipated power.

It was not long before Italy, with its centers of music in the ecclesiastical and operatic fields, beckoned strongly to Herr Mozart, because it offered a very necessary background for Wolfgang's training. But it was not until the lad was nearly fourteen that father and son set out for Italy.

That he was still very much a boy in spite of his precocity is seen in his letter to his home, written in Naples:

"Please write to me soon and every post day. I thank you for having sent me the arithmetic books and beg you, if you ever wish for me to have a headache, to send me a few more of these examples."

As stanch Catholics, the Mozarts wished particularly to visit the city of Rome. Here it was that Wolfgang performed a memory feat so distinguished that it has become a classic story of genius. They reached the city during a thunderstorm. Wolfgang made much of this when he wrote home, that they had been "received like great men with the firing of heavy guns." On Wednesday of Holy Week they went to the Sistine Chapel and heard Allegri's *Miserere*. This great work was regarded as so sacred that it had never been written down in score and to write it was forbidden. A violation would mean excommunication.

Wolfgang listened. Every note of the sacred score imprinted itself indelibly on his fertile mind. After the service they hastened to their room, and Wolfgang wrote down the entire score "for five choruses with a nine-part finale" by memory. News of what he had accomplished spread abroad and soon reached the pope. The latter was so astonished at the lad's genius that instead of excommunicating him, the pontiff conferred on him the order of The Golden Spurs.

Darkening and ominous clouds already began to gather over young Mozart's head. Less frequently did the sunshine of friendship and success break through. Honor and gifts were not lacking; but the wherewithal of existence, patronage, a position, haunted his future days. He had so much to give to the world. All he asked was the "liberty" to create for mankind.

A family council. Another tour. But Herr Mozart could not break loose from his moorings at Salzburg. It was decided that Wolfgang and his mother should go, and father would steer their course by letter. Money was hurriedly borrowed for the young artist. Besides the incidental expenses, he must keep up appearances.

Father eagerly awaited their first letter. It came from Munich. He tore it open only to find that Wolfgang's effort to lay himself and his services most humbly at the elector's feet had been unsuccessful.

At Mannheim, Wolfgang was introduced to Herr Weber, also a musician, and a handy man at the court opera. The Webers were poor in worldly goods but rich in the love of music and in comely daughters. Josepha, the eldest daughter, had a fine, although untrained, voice. Aloysia, next, also gave musical promise. Then there were vivacious Constance and Sophie, who was only ten. When the young and eligible artist paid a visit to their home, he dropped with characteristic ease the carefreighted errand of his trip to enjoy to the full the drafts of mirth and song and friendliness of this humble home.

Aloysia sang. Wolfgang accompanied. They soared together on the wings of music. The composer took a special delight in hearing the young soprano sing one of his own arias. He was charmed by her singing. He was charmed, too, by the singer. All too quickly the evening ended, but Wolfgang had become intoxicated with the perfume of love. He returned to his lodging walking on air. Aloysia! Ah, Aloysia!

He burst into his mother's room to break the news of—a position? a patron? No! he had found a lovely pearl! Just as quickly his mother burst the bubble of his fancy. He must wait with such things. Meanwhile she would secretly write father for counsel.

Mother Mozart knew the cogent force behind the rhythm of fluttering hearts, with its accelerating tempos, rising crescendos, and sudden climaxes. She would check the flow of this rhapsodic music, inserting bars of time and distance, lest the overture of their lives close abruptly in a deceptive cadence. Father likewise did his share to prune the bud of romance in several lengthy, impassioned letters. "Off with you to Paris," he wrote, "and that immediately!"

So the heartsick youth yielded, and indifferently helped his mother to pack their baggage to leave Mannheim and his dream for Paris and mundane affairs. During the ten-day journey, Wolfgang, preoccupied, said very little. He was struggling with mixed feelings: Was he not twenty-one and of man's estate? On the other hand, he realized his duties as a loving son.

Humble lodgings were procured in Paris, and Wolfgang set out to make contacts with several scores of influential people—hoping for a commission or an appointment. Unfortunately, the Gluck-Puccini controversy was at its height at this time, with musical society divided into two factions, thus causing other composers, including Mozart, to be ignored.

He returned one evening from another futile search, to find his mother very ill. He tenderly nursed her and did all he could to relieve her suffering, but she became steadily worse. The doctor was called. He prescribed one of the strange concoctions of the time, but she only weakened. The end seemed imminent. A priest came and administered the last rites. Wolfgang kept a constant vigil at her bedside. "I prayed to God for two things only," he wrote later, "a happy death hour for my mother, and then for myself strength and courage." She died in his arms.

Wolfgang was left with the doubly sad task of burying his mother in a strange land, and breaking the news to his father as gently as possible. At the close of one of his letters to his father he wrote: "Let us submit ourselves steadfastly to the divine will, fully convinced it will be for our good, for He does all things well."

He stayed on in Paris for some time, hoping against hope that his quest for permanent work would be realized. But as his purse became leaner, his confidence sank, and he resolved at length to return to Salzburg. He looked forward to one bright spot on his return trip—a visit to the Weber family. Again he was doomed to disappointment, for Aloysia, having received the attention of another, and also an operatic appointment, met him coldly.

Six months had passed since Mozart had left his home and a rather insignificant position in the service of the archbishop, to sally forth to conquer the hearts of men. He returned a tired warrior, having lost every engagement—his mother, his first love, and the hope of a better position.

Through these bitter experiences, as well as through the brighter ones of his life, Mozart's art flourished, and he continued to compose copiously from seemingly unlimited resources. His life was like a gorgeous flower whose fragrance became more profuse as it was crushed deeper and deeper under the feet of careless men. His pen flew with uncanny rapidity across the staffs. Once when sending a prelude and fugue to his sister, he apologized for a lack of neatness in copying, inasmuch as he had written the fugue while composing the prelude. By the time he was twenty-four, he had written nearly four hundred works, in all forms, including masses, operas, concertos, and string quartets.

The archbishop, with whom Mozart had now gained employment as choirmaster and organist, had gone to Vienna, and soon thereafter summoned the composer to join him. Mozart appeared there at public and private concerts and was received with the greatest enthusiasm. Meanwhile he had to eat at the servants' table, and suffered many indignities at the hands of the prelate. Finally, in a verbal encounter, the composer dared to assert his rights—the docile lamb became a roaring lion, archbishop or no archbishop. Ultimately, Mozart resigned. When he asked for his dismissal, the steward contributed the culminating gesture when he seized Mozart and literally kicked him out of the room.

As soon as the mortified young man regained his composure, his first thought, on wondering where to go next, was of the Weber family. Although Herr Weber had died and Aloysia had left home to marry an actor, Mozart knew that this was one home where he was loved and understood.

The congenial atmosphere of the Weber home contrasted so strongly with that of the archbishop's household that the lonely, discouraged composer soon succumbed under its friendly spell. His letters to his father took on a persuasive tone. "To my mind a bachelor lives only half a life," he wrote. And now who was the object of his attention? Constance, Aloysia's next-younger sister. When after many months he led her to the altar, the happy bridegroom confided: "I am just beginning to live."

And now there were two to chase the phantom of security. They were certainly "birds of a feather," for she was as impractical in the management of financial matters as was he. They moved a dozen times in nine years of married life, seeking the pot of gold at the end of the tri-colored rainbow of prestige, patronage, and position.

The two paths of Mozart's life, material success and creative production, diverged farther and farther, the one ending in a wilderness of financial trouble and despair, the other becoming greater and grander, and culminating in masterpieces of unsurpassed splendor.

The young couple began housekeeping in Vienna on nearly nothing. Mozart seemed to have thought that marriage would solve all his economic problems; but with the dawn of each new day he learned afresh that two times nothing is still nothing. Not that Mozart was indolent. Rather, he was unusually industrious; and he was honest. But he was sadly impractical and lacking in principles of expediency and diplomacy. Moreover, he was a victim of the vicious policy of the times whereby musicians were at the mercy of the whims of royalty, and composers were forced by circumstances to sell the birthright of their creations for a "mess of pottage." Some of his greatest works, such as *Don Juan* and *Figaro*, each netted him the small sum of two hundred dollars.

Listen as he confides to his father: "I could go around Vienna looking like a tramp, but I must not. My linen is pitiable. No servant has shirts of such coarse stuff as mine—and certainly that is a frightful thing for a man with pride." He took to giving lessons, against his own inclinations. "I now have two scholars," he wrote one of his friends. "I would like to bring the number to eight." And in conclusion he pleads, "Try to spread it abroad that I am giving lessons, will you, please?" A prophet—unknown.

He had some faithful friends, but surpassing them all was the mutual bond of love and appreciation between him and Haydn. In a visit with the young composer and his father, Haydn took the latter aside and said, "I declare to you before God as a man of honor, that your son is the greatest composer that I know, either personally or by reputation; he has taste, and beyond that the most consummate knowledge of the art of composition." On the other hand, Mozart's sincere admiration of Haydn was shown when, after having dedicated six quartets to Haydn, he added, "This was only my duty, for I learned from Haydn how to write quartets." And on another occasion he turned to another composer in his company and said in reply to a slightly derogatory remark that the other composer made regarding Haydn, "If they melt us both together, there will not yet be stuff enough to make a real Haydn."

Although the two geniuses were opposites in many respects,

they were kindred spirits. Haydn, twenty-four years older than Mozart, was for a time his teacher; but the teacher was free to acknowledge the younger artist as his model in certain fields. Where Haydn was methodical and shrewd, Mozart was prodigal and unbusinesslike. Haydn was the simple, happy peasant, whereas Mozart was the gallant and witty man of the world. Musically, Haydn was slow in his development, whereas Mozart matured very rapidly. Together they enlarged the classical forms and styles, and enriched orchestral coloring.

Mozart's greatness reached into many fields of composition; he was one of the finest of melodists, and he was a forceful dramatic composer. In passage work his delicate pen seems to trace a fountain spray or to chase a zephyr on a summer's day. His style is a model of refinement, taste, and crystal clarity. More than a thousand works, some of which require a whole evening to perform, came from his pen.

The path of his pursuit for daily bread became narrower and was flanked increasingly by creditors, for he had to maintain his home on a 'sporadic income, with his wife ill almost constantly. Two of his four children died.

Meanwhile, the path of his creative growth widened with each passing year. Rare flowers, exotic plants, towering trees, grew abundantly. Within six weeks he wrote his three great symphonies, the *E-flat major, G minor,* and *C minor,* or *Jupiter Symphony.* The operas, *The Magic Flute, Figaro,* and *Don Giovanni* (the overture of the last-named having been written in a single evening), were also members of this giant forest of masterly compositions.

Mozart, now aged though but a youth, poor although he had unlimited resources, hungry while his music was to feed the multitudes, became wasted in body and weary in soul.

A stranger—gaunt, somberly clad, sober of mien—knocked at Mozart's door. He handed the composer a message and departed. It proved to be a commission for the composer to write a *Requiem.* A price satisfactory to Mozart was stipulated, but the name of the patron was not divulged.

He began to write the mass. But somehow as he composed, a strange feeling came over him. Who was the stranger? Who was his patron? For whose death was he composing?

His work on the *Requiem* was interrupted for a short time, as it was necessary for him to leave for Prague to write an opera there for the occasion of the crowning of Emperor Leopold II. Just as he was about to step into the carriage the mysterious stranger appeared and touched him on the arm. He inquired where Mozart was going. "What about the *Requiem?*" he asked. The composer blanched and stammered some excuses and promised to return soon. The stranger left, and Mozart proceeded on his way. But throughout the journey the vision of the stranger seemed to haunt the composer and filled his mind with sinister forebodings.

He resumed work on the *Requiem* even though he was fast becoming physically exhausted and was laboring under heavy mental strain. He took to his bed, but continued to compose the mass. A presentiment of death came over him; he became obsessed with the idea that he was writing the mass for himself. Doubtless it was these aberrations that hastened his end; the notes of the scores became to him the black darts of fate. (The identity of the stranger and of the patron of the *Requiem* later became known, but the composer never learned it.) Malignant typhus fever further ravaged his exhausted frame, and he died with the *Requiem*—near at hand—unfinished.

On a blustering December day, Mozart, a youth of thirty-five winters, whose musical legacy to the world pictured eternal spring, was carried to his rest. Constance Mozart was confined to her bed at the time, and the few mourners who accompanied the body turned back at the city's gates because of the bitter weather. In a lonely spot—without one note of music—he was buried in a pauper's grave.

He died destitute—but he enriched the world.

Ludwig van Beethoven

1770-1827

Poet and Peasant

◦

HE close of the eighteenth century witnessed the rise of a new era in the concepts and ideals of men. The American forefathers had declared for independence and freedom. From France had risen the cry: "Liberty, Fraternity, Equality." Champions of democratic ideals arose in fields of commerce and invention, of literature and art.

In this period of revolution and assertion of equal rights appeared a man whose genius, courage, and love of liberty were to revolutionize music. He was to break the fetters of formalism and set music free. Not satisfied to view the symmetry and balance of the body of music, he penetrated into its soul.

Bonn-on-the-Rhine, Germany, famous for its university and beautiful environs, was the birthplace of Ludwig van Beethoven. He was born in 1770, the same year in which Wordsworth, famed in literary history as a reformer and a leader in the romantic movement, was born, and one year after the birth of Napoleon Bonaparte, Corsican militarist, whose ambitious conquests, and defeats, loomed large in European political history during the lifetime of the composer.

Ludwig was born in a little, dingy attic room. His ancestry was mottled in shades of dark and light. His paternal grand-

51

Ludwig van Beethoven

father, a highly respected man, became well to do in the wine business. Unfortunately, his wife became too deeply interested in the business for her own good, for she became addicted to strong drink and it was necessary for her to spend her last days in an institution. Ludwig's father inherited this weakness of character, and often Ludwig and his brothers would have to carry their drunken father home after one of his sprees. He was, moreover, improvident, and sometimes cruel. Ludwig's mother, on the other hand, was soft spoken, patient, and orderly.

Ludwig was not a prodigy, but as soon as his father discovered that there was some talent in his son, he decided that he would make of him a second Mozart, and shift some of his own responsibility to Ludwig as a second provider for the home. Herr van Beethoven was employed as a musician at the archbishop-elector's court at a miserable salary, and he used his fair knowledge of music to give Ludwig his first lessons when his son was only four. He proved a severe taskmaster and often Ludwig's tears would mix with his music.

Neighborhood boys nicknamed him "the Spaniard," because of his swarthy complexion, and sometimes it was "the mad Spaniard," because of his flights of temper. His "broad shoulders, short neck, thick head, round nose, blackish-brown complexion," gave the picture of a prospective wrestler rather than of a promising musician. His boyhood days were unhappy. The harsh treatment he received at the hands of his intemperate, irascible father doubtless laid the foundation for the morose and sarcastic traits that developed in his own character. What tender care he received from his mother was early broken off, for she died of tuberculosis when Ludwig was seventeen.

Ludwig stopped school at eleven. In music he passed from one teacher to another, most of whom failed to recognize him as a budding genius. Albrechtsberger, his teacher in composition, prophesied: "Beethoven never has learned anything and never will learn anything. As a composer he is hopeless," Haydn, too, with whom Ludwig studied over a short period, showed little sympathy with the radical tendencies of his pupil. Mozart, how-

ever, was astonished on hearing Ludwig improvise, and exclaimed, "Take notice of him . . . ; he will make a noise in the
world." While still in his early teens Ludwig received an organ
post, first without pay, and later became a member of the elector
of Cologne's orchestra, with a small salary.

Shortly after his mother died, Ludwig became intimate with
a fine cultivated family of Bonn, the Von Breunings. He gave
lessons to the son and daughter, and became just like a member of
the family. Mother Von Breuning was especially adept at handling the impetuous youth. "He is again in his *raptus,*" she would
say when he experienced one of his sudden flares of temper. Ludwig never forgot this expression. "She understood how to keep
the insects from the flowers," he later remarked. Here Ludwig
became intimately acquainted with the literature of his country and of England. Here, too, he met Count Waldstein, who was
instrumental in helping to bring out genius and to whom Beethoven dedicated his *Waldstein Sonata, Opus* 53.

It was Count Waldstein who arranged that Ludwig should
go to Vienna and study with Haydn. In the album given to
Ludwig as a farewell gift, Waldstein wrote: "Dear Beethoven,
you are traveling to Vienna in fulfillment of your long-cherished
wish. The genius of Mozart is still weeping and bewailing the
death of her favorite. With the inexhaustible Haydn she found
a refuge, but no occupation, and is now waiting to leave him and
join herself to someone else. Labor assiduously and receive
Mozart's spirit from the hands of Haydn."

On the journey from Bonn he jotted notes of interest and
items of expense in a notebook. This was the nucleus of what
became a habit with him, and led to the sketchbook process
of composing. In this notebook he recorded his musical ideas,
and later developed them. He was twenty-two when he arrived
in Vienna, taking his first lodging in a garret. He had hardly
settled when he received, in quick succession, news that his
father had died by his own hand, and that Ludwig's allowance
from the elector of Cologne had ceased. These changes left the
young man entirely on his own resources.

As with Haydn and Mozart, Beethoven found a haven in the palatial residence of a prince. Unlike them, however, Beethoven did not allow his independent spirit to be cowed by a sense of the superiority of the prince's station—his peasant birth notwithstanding. *"Here* and *here* is my nobility," he once remarked as he pointed to his head and heart. On another occasion a friend with whom he had visited the court turned to him as they were returning home and said, "I am glad that you knew the proper etiquette in the presence of the nobility." "You ought to be glad that the nobility knew the proper etiquette in the presence of genius," was Beethoven's pungent reply.

In spite of his contemptuous attitude toward the aristocracy, they consistently overlooked his brusque exterior and appreciated the sincerity and the simplicity of his motives. Furthermore, many members of the royal families were musical amateurs and were willing to sacrifice breaches of etiquette in order to foster the products of his genius.

Beethoven's creative powers matured slowly, especially when compared with the fecundity of Mozart. Mozart's first symphony was written when he was eight, whereas Beethoven's first symphony was composed when he was thirty. Naturally the disparity in their ages is evident in the two symphonies.

Nature was Beethoven's workshop. Sketchbook in hand, he wandered for hours in the open country, there to undergo the birth throes of his masterworks. A peasant friend who lived for a time with the master relates of his daily habits: "At half past seven was the family breakfast, and directly after it he hurried out of doors and sauntered about the fields, calling out, waving his hands, going now very slowly, then very fast, and then suddenly standing still and writing in a kind of pocketbook. At half past twelve he came into the house to dinner, and after dinner he went to his own room till three or so, then again in the fields till about sunset." The master expressed the response of nature to the cravings of his soul and the loftiness of his thoughts in the following poetic language: "In the country every tree seems to talk to me saying 'Holy! Holy!' In the forest is enchantment which expresses all things—sweet peace of the forest! Almighty, I am happy in the woods, blessed in the woods, every tree has a voice through Thee. O God, what glory in such a woodland place! On the heights is peace—peace to serve Thee. How glad am I once again to be able to wander in forest and thicket among the trees, the green things, and the rocks. No mortal can love the country as I do; for woods and trees and rocks return the echo a man desires."

He was singularly fond of water. He enjoyed pouring it over his head and wrists until, at times, the floor of his room became flooded and the water seeped through the ceiling underneath, and only the remonstrances of his neighbors below would bring him out of his reverie. If perchance, while on one of his country strolls, he was caught in a thundershower, he seemed entirely oblivious of the downpour and continued to jot down his music ideas until the sketchbook became too soaked to use.

In the *Pastoral Symphony* Beethoven expresses in tone his tribute to nature as a manifestation of God. The movements progress through the following descriptive changes: 1. Awakening of cheerful emotions on arriving in the country. 2. Scene by the brook. 3. Peasants' merrymaking. 4. Thunderstorm, tempest. 5. Shepherd's hymn, happy and thankful feelings after the storm.

Music of this type is called "program music" as contrasted with abstract or absolute music. Program music may be of several styles. In the *Pastoral Symphony* Beethoven intended "no picture, but something in which the emotions are expressed which are aroused in men by the pleasure of the country." Many composers, including those of the first rank, such as Handel and Haydn, have, on the other hand, sought to depict realistic scenes, as when the former in his oratorio, *Israel in Egypt*, imitates the hopping of frogs.

In connection with program music the subject of fantastic stories that have evolved about certain pieces naturally arises. A case in point is Beethoven's *Moonlight Sonata*. Many legends have gathered around this, perhaps the most famous of the master's works, and they are often so prettily pathetic that it seems cruel to "denude" them. Nevertheless, it is a matter of historical fact that the composer did not give this sonata a title. Any of the stories concerning this beautiful work are but fiction.

Beethoven's *Third Symphony* had its inspiration in historic events of the first decade of the nineteenth century. The gallant figure of Napoleon appealed to the composer as an apostle of freedom, and his *Eroica* (Heroic) *Symphony* was dedicated to his republican idol; but when he learned that Napoleon was an absolutist at heart and had been crowned emperor, he became enraged and tore up the title page bearing the name Napoleon Bonaparte, and stamped it under his feet. He then wrote a new title page which read, "Composed to celebrate the memory of a great man." In keeping with the initial dedication the composer declared for freedom of musical thought. He severed the "apron strings" with which he was tied to Haydn and Mozart. He launched out into uncharted seas—defiant of the winds of criticism—with bolder harmonies, finer orchestral coloring, and a new conception of the importance of the emotions in music. It was the fulfillment of an earlier resolve: "I am dissatisfied with my previous works; from today forth I am going to strike forth into a new path."

In these days of dictatorship and tyranny the voice of the liberty-loving Beethoven rises with renewed emphasis, and his *Fifth Symphony* has become a symbol of victory to men and women everywhere, and especially to those living in the shadows of lurking despots. The rhythmic motive of the symphony, the same as that of the letter V in the Morse telegraphic code—three dots and a dash (... —), occurs over one hundred times in the first movement. The program of the stirring *Fifth* is as follows:

First movement—outer struggle
Second movement—repose, comfort, reassurance
Third movement—inner struggle
Fourth movement—final victory

The *Fifth Symphony* represented, moreover, an inner struggle in the life of the composer. As a young man of twenty-eight, Beethoven began having trouble with his hearing. At first he became morbidly sensitive and sought solitude, in order to avoid embarrassment in associating with people, but after several years he took a more philosophical attitude toward his malady and decided that he "must get out and lustily knock about the world." And "knock about" he did.

Of all the dispensers of music's jewels, Beethoven holds a unique position in the particularly fastidious care he lavished on his artistic productions. The embryonic ideas of his masterpieces changed their shape sometimes forty or fifty times before they were adopted into the finished product. He polished, refined, set, and reset musical gems until each facet reached a distinctive luster. Then he placed these precious stones, each complementing the other, until a veritable jewelhouse of tone was built. Beethoven carried the *Ninth (Choral) Symphony* in his mind for thirty years before it was completed.

The master was frequently in love, but his ardent wooing and fervent proposals were lost on deaf ears. The favored ones preferred the intense passion and tender lyricism of his music to that of his love. They knew that he was becoming increasingly cynical; that he was absent-minded and eccentric. They knew him as a man *in* the world, but not *of* it.

When Beethoven's brother died leaving a nine-year-old son, the master assumed responsibility for the lad and eventually adopted him. The relationship proved most unfortunate. An overzealous, impetuous uncle and an ungrateful, worthless nephew can make life for one another most miserable. But to the close of his life Beethoven continued to lavish a bearish affection on the boy and received in return a rascal's disdain.

It is assumed that the care of his nephew Carl and his own deafness weighed heavily on the spirit of Beethoven, and contributed to his untimely death at fifty-six. While returning from a country visit to a brother, he caught a cold. Complications set in that sent him to his bed. His final struggle lasted for two days. In his dying hours Franz Schubert visited him, coming as it were to fill his own censer with the smoldering embers from the hand of the dying master. In contrast with the solitary burial of Mozart, Beethoven's passing was mourned by all Vienna. Upwards of twenty thousand people attended his funeral.

Beethoven's life and works, like Shakespeare's, fall naturally into three periods or manners. The first period begins in the styles of Haydn and Mozart and includes many early sonatas, the first two symphonies, and the first three piano concertos. In the second period there is a breaking away from precedent and an increasing tendency toward self-expression. This period includes the *Waldstein* and *Appassionata* sonatas, the *G major* and *E-flat major* piano concertos, and the *Eroica Symphony*. In the last period his genius reaches full flower. His afflicted, tried, and saddened spirit finds expression in some of the most profound and sublime music that has come from the pen of mortal men. His latest sonatas, quartets, and the *Choral Symphony* were creations of this period.

Beethoven's life and music are inseparable. His humor and wit are mirrored in the playful scherzos, his fickle temperament in sudden dynamic changes, and the tragedy and deep feeling of his life in the slow movements. And his music continues to fill a vital need in life today. The nobility, the sincerity, the natural beauty of his thoughts find a response in an ever-widening circle of music lovers as the years of his sojourn recede into the distant past and the sadness of his life becomes but a memory.

A retrospective parting glimpse of the music master pictures him again in his young manhood, after the hand of affliction had closed to him the door of the world of sound. He held the key to chambers of rare and delightful music for others to enter and enjoy, while he himself must remain without. In pensive mood he soliloquized, "I have emptied the cup of bitter suffering." Then, magnanimous in heart and invincible in spirit, he resolved: "It shall be transformed into beauty in my soul. . . . I owe it to myself, to mankind, and to the Almighty. . . . I must write my music . . . to the eternal glory of God."

The master kept his resolve.

Franz Schubert

1797-1828

"He was a very little man, but he was a giant"

～

Such a lovely melody has come into my head, if I had
but some music paper." In these words Franz Schubert gives, in
essence, the fabulous gifts and extreme penury of his life. He was
a musician of regal rank in the tattered garments of an indigent
peasant; his was an incomparable genius for melody, a spontaneous gift for song, but alas! he was often too poor to purchase
the paper on which to pen his musical thoughts.

Franz Schubert had just taken a Sunday afternoon stroll with
some of his friends. They were passing a beer garden, when they
recognized another friend sitting at a table. They entered. As
Schubert seated himself he picked up a book that was lying near
at hand. It happened to be a volume of Shakespeare. As he casu-
ally thumbed through the pages of the play *Cymbeline* his eye
was caught by the lines:

> "Hark, hark! the lark at heaven's gate sings,
> And Phoebus 'gins arise—"

The euphony, the suggestive freshness, the joyous rhythm of
the opening lines touched his fancy. He read on:

60

"His steeds to water at those springs
On chalic'd flowers that lies;
And winking marybuds begin
To ope their golden eyes;
With everything that pretty is:
My lady sweet, arise;
Arise, arise!"

He had no sooner finished reading the lines than its musical poetry became transformed into poetic music. But, as usual, this sudden sunshower of melody caught him without paper or pen. One of his cronies drew some staves on the back of a bill of fare, passed it over to Schubert and presently, "Hark! Hark! the Lark," one of the most charming songs ever written, was given its miraculous birth.

Franz was one of fourteen children in the family of Schoolmaster Schubert and his wife, who had been a cook before her marriage. While Father Schubert loved music and was an amateur musician, there was seemingly no trace of musical royalty in the blood of Franz's forebears. Herr Schubert was conscientious, hard-working, and poor; Frau Schubert was a good mother, quiet and God-fearing. But her sweet influence was not long to bless the home; she died of typhus in 1812, when Franz was fifteen.

Franz was born in Lichtenthal, a district of Vienna. Vienna! where lies your charm that gifted sons should choose to bide within your gates? Foster sons—Haydn, Mozart, Beethoven; and now a native son—Schubert. Was it your bounty? Some starved well-nigh to death! Was it your peace? The tramp of soldiers' feet came to their very doors; and the bursting throats of Napoleon's guns disgorged their deadly potions. Was it your freedom? Ah, no! for liberty of speech and action was suppressed, and voices became muted, and silence was their echo. Was it your love of art and literature? Even here the tide was low. And still we seek, *Wien,* the magic of your spell. Perhaps the wisdom of your years decreed that your greatest sons must "pass through the fires of affliction" that only the pure gold of their worth should remain, to stand the stress and strain of changing generations.

Franz received his first music on the clavier and violin from his father and an older brother. But his natural talent soon ran ahead of that of his teachers, and the choirmaster of the parish was engaged to carry on. How the new teacher reveled in his musical trust is easily imagined. "When I wished to teach him anything fresh," he once said, "he always knew it already. I have often listened to him in astonishment."

In his twelfth year Franz was sent to the Jesuit school. At first the other boys teased him because of his conspicuous home-spun clothes, but this soon ceased when they heard his beautiful soprano voice and his gift of natural expression. The boys were taught grammar and mathematics (here Franz did not excel) and other rudiments. The choir prepared them for the Court Chapel and many were members of the school orchestra. When Franz first played his violin in the orchestra, a large boy in front of him turned about to see who was playing so cleverly behind him. His eyes met the shy glance of bespectacled little Franz. The two became fast friends. Soon Franz modestly acknowledged that he wrote music when he had paper on which to write. And his new-found friend thereafter saw to it that paper was at hand whenever the Muse would knock at Schubert's door.

Another of his schoolmates gave an intimate glimpse of the boy Franz as he knew him: "When I came into closer touch with Schubert, he was in the fourth grammar form, a short, sturdy boy with a friendly round face and strongly marked features. He was not a particular favorite of the clerical professors, yet he was no particular trouble to them by excessive liveliness. He proved that he possessed one of those quiet, deep minds which made superficial pedagogues misjudge his silent nature as a sign of little talent."

Living conditions at the school were not the best. The rooms were insufficiently heated and the food was scant. When Franz could stand it no longer, he sat down at his little table and wrote to his brother Ferdinand, who was three years older:

"I've been thinking for a long while about my position, and

find that in most respects it is good; in others it could be improved upon. You know from experience that a roll or an apple, or more, can be enjoyed after an eight and a half hours' fast, with only a wretched supper to look forward to. This need has become so pressing that I must change it. The two *groschen* my father sends me are gone in a few days. If, therefore, I have to depend upon you I hope I may do so without feeling ashamed. So I thought: How would it be if you were to advance me a couple of *kreutzers* monthly? You would never miss them, whilst I should shut myself in my cell, and be quite happy. As the apostle Paul says: 'Let him that hath two coats give one to the poor.'"

But even in these teen years, and in spite of hardships, his compositions went on apace. In contrast with his mode of living, they were neither scant nor poor. "It was interesting to see him compose." So wrote a schoolmate in a letter. "Very rarely did he use the piano. He often said that would interrupt the train of his thoughts. Quietly and little troubled by the talking and noise of his fellow students—unavoidable at the convent [school] —he sat at his little table, a sheet of note paper in front of him, and closely stooped over that and the textbook (he was very shortsighted), chewing the pen, sometimes playing (as if trying a passage) with his fingers on the table, and writing easily and fluently without many corrections, as if it had to be just so, and not otherwise."

Owing to his change of voice at fifteen, Franz could no longer sing soprano in the choir. On the flyleaf of one of his schoolbooks, still preserved, is scribbled in a boy's hand:

"Franz Schubert has crowed for the last time,
July 26, 1812."

His mother, "the good mother," as Franz affectionately wrote of her in his diary, died this same year. A year later Schoolmaster Schubert married again. There were five more children. This brought the number up to nineteen. The stepmother cheerfully filled the breach left by the mother's passing. She had a habit of placing any small savings in a stocking. Franz knew too well of the "woolen" bank. "Anything in the stocking, Mother?" he would ask when his own stocking failed him. The quest was generally rewarded.

For several years Franz taught in his father's school, although the routine of the classroom was distasteful to him. However, he chose this in preference to military conscription, inasmuch as teachers were given exemption by the government. But during the hours spent in the drudgery of cramming numbers and letters into "hollow" heads, he looked forward to the evening when he could relax in melodic expression. That he was unable to appreciate the noble and satisfying side of teaching, accepting it rather as a grinding chore, is understandable in the light of his spontaneous nature as contrasted with the phlegmatic temperaments he must certainly have met in many of his pupils.

The seventeen-year-old teacher seemed to reflect his attitude toward his duties when he wrote the mournful song, "Margaret at the Spinning Wheel." Margaret, a character from Goethe's *Faust*, in a mood of sadness over bitter memories and lost hopes, laments her fate:

> "My peace is gone, my heart oppressed,
>   And never again will my soul find rest."

At any rate, the experience the young composer gained in contact with life in the schoolroom enabled him to grasp the spirit of this and similar poems and give them a new and deeper meaning in his particularly congruous musical settings.

On a winter afternoon in 1815, the little schoolmaster, having dismissed his classes for the day, sat in his schoolroom reading selections from Goethe. His interest became intense and impassioned as he read "The Erlking," a ballad based on a legend of the Black Forest in Baden. It is a story of a father riding horseback on a stormy night. He holds his little son close to his breast and rides furiously toward home. But in close pursuit follows the erlking, seeking to beguile the child and to snatch him from the father's embrace. The tempest rages, the child shrieks in terror, the rider madly spurs his horse to greater speed. At last they see the light in their window. A few more steps and they are home. The door is closed. But alas! when security is reached, the father is horrified to see, by the glow of the hearth fire, that his son is dead.

Schubert's old friend Spaun, who had first provided the composer with music paper at the Jesuit school, happened to call just as Schubert had finished reading "The Erlking." Spaun knocked, but there was no answer; so he entered—to find Schubert pacing the floor in rapturous thought. The composer then sat down and quickly wrote out the dramatic musical accompaniment which was to become known as his greatest song. It was played and sung the same evening by a group of friends, with divergent opinions as to its worth. Some considered it too bold and dissonant. Publishers refused, at first, to publish it. Even Goethe failed to recognize the superior quality of the music, but time has proved its classic worth, and the ballad itself has become universally known by virtue of its being wedded to the music.

Schubert wrote more than six hundred songs. He had but to touch a poem and it seemed to turn to music. He chose his texts from Shakespeare, Goethe, and Schiller. More than sixty poems from Goethe alone were set to music. "He could have set a placard to music," said Schumann. And always, that close affinity between words and music is a striking feature of his art. The darting, gliding accompaniment to "The Trout" would seem to tempt any angler. His song "Thou Art Repose" breathes a spirit of peace; his "Faith in Spring" generates hope. "Ave Maria," "Serenade," "The Wanderer"— what an array of musical portraits make up his gallery!

Schubert was insignificant looking. He was just slightly over five feet tall—stoutish, with fat arms and stubby fingers. His hair was black and curly, his complexion pasty. Heavy eyebrows arched his piercing eyes. His small glasses seemed to fit his face much as children would hang an old pair of spectacles on a snowman's nose. He was round-shouldered, and was often seen walking with head bowed, and hands behind his back as if lost in thought.

5

But despite his unpretentious personal appearance he drew about him a circle of faithful friends. Good-natured, truthful, altruistic, he seemed to exert a charm over those he met that won their hearts. Poets, musicians, painters, rallied round him and formed a coterie, calling themselves the Schubertiads, frequently meeting together in true Bohemian style. When a guest appeared at one of these gatherings, Schubert invariably asked, "Can he do anything?" So something more than a mere password was required to gain membership in this elite group. Schubert's frivolous side came to light here also. His favorite vaudeville stunt was his singing of his "Erlking" through a fine-toothed comb. The esteem with which Schubert was held by the members of the circle was expressed by Vogl, a fine baritone, when the young master was late for an appointment. "We must all bend before Schubert's genius," said he, "and if he does not come, we must creep after him on our knees."

If it had not been for these friends, what would have become of Schubert is a matter for conjecture. Except for the three years spent in teaching in his father's school and a short time spent as a sort of music servant in the household of Esterhazy, he was never regularly employed. If Schubert had been given a government pension, such as our present-day Sibelius obtains from the Finnish Government, we can but imagine what would have been the results. While spiritual values cannot be weighed in any human scale of weights or measures, certainly a life as precious as Schubert's for the good of mankind, deserves not only the pension of a government but of a world. When publishers swindled the gullible composer, he turned to his friends. When he loved, and lost, he turned to his friends. Unrequited labor, unrequited love. Fortunately for the world, he had some friends.

Not all of the associations formed, however, were of the best, and these proved the master's undoing, for the habit of drink and other excesses led to an early illness and to his untimely death. The first signs of illness came when he was twenty-five. In 1823 he spent a number of weeks in a hospital. He was discharged, but the symptoms recurred, together with spells of despondency. Even the qualifications of genius cannot bring salvation to a man, but he, as all men, must depend on a higher power for sustaining grace.

Though he was handicapped by the broken pinions of illhealth, his songs took wing to bluer skies and fairer fields. "My music," said Schubert, "is the product of my genius and my misery, and that which I have written in my greatest distress is that which the world seems to like the best."

Then the friendship circle broke. Some of the group married; others left Vienna for distant parts. Except for occasional visits from old friends, Schubert was alone. An added blow to the waning spirit of the young genius came when Beethoven died in 1827. Franz was a torchbearer in the funeral procession of his idol, and was endowed to bear the "musical torch" after the death of the master of Bonn. Little did he realize that his own life's flame was to go out in just another year.

In his thirty-second year he moved to his brother's home, in order to better his health in the quiet of nature's byways. But he failed to rally and soon thereafter contracted typhus. In spite of the attention of several physicians and the most tender nursing care, his life thread broke while he lay in his brother's arms. The master of the *Unfinished Symphony,* in the full flush of his creative powers, and at the threshold of greater promise, had abruptly closed his unfinished career. Inscribed on his tombstone was the appropriate epitaph:

> "Music has here buried a rich treasure,
> But much fairer hopes."

Schubert takes his place in music history as a supreme lyric composer—the greatest of song writers. The short span of his life, together with the fact that he was the least educated of the masters, served to circumscribe his genius. All things being equal, he might have been the greatest of them all. We know he lacked the attitude of meticulous care that Beethoven exercised in the constant revision and perfection of his works. As a result, especially in his larger works, Schubert is likely to ramble, and some of his works seem to be lacking in proportion. This again may be a point of view. For Schumann, his *C-major Symphony* was of "heavenly length." He had hoped and tried for success in the operatic field—and failed. Although many of his symphonies and sonatas retain their hold as classic masterpieces, it is in the field of song and in the smaller forms such as the Impromptus, Moment Musicals, etc., that he singularly excelled.

To Schubert, music was as the breath of life. "He was over-joyed," wrote a close friend, "when beautiful music was performed. He folded his hands and placed them against his mouth and sat there as if in ecstasy." He reveled in the works of the older masters, and the masterpieces of Mozart seemed, above all others, to touch the wellsprings of his heart. His words concerning Mozart's music, as gleaned from his diary, are, moreover, a tribute to all good music:

"Gently, as if out of the distance, did the magic touch of Mozart's music touch my ears. Such lovely impressions remain on the soul, there to work for good, past all power of time or circumstances. In the darkness of this life they reveal a clear, bright, beautiful prospect, inspiring confidence and hope."

Felix Mendelssohn-Bartholdy

1809-1847

From Jewish Lad to Christian
Apostle of Pure and Living Music

～～

HE STOOD waiting by the Rosenthaler Gate at the entrance to Berlin. Even his name, Moses Mendelssohn, was against him. For centuries many of his people had been oppressed and persecuted, stalked like animals of prey, and ruthlessly slain. Others were taxed unreasonably by the state and taunted by religionists of other faiths.

The fourteen-year-old penniless Jewish boy, small and deformed in body, stammered his replies to the official at the gate, and at last gained entrance into the city.

Moses' outward appearance belied his clear-thinking mind and charm of character. He had come to the city to learn. Food was of passing importance; he marked off a loaf of bread to last the week. He bent every energy to the study of languages, philosophy, and mathematics, until he became in time a great philosopher in his own right and was to be known eventually as the Jewish Socrates.

In the course of time Moses married. Six children were born, all of whom inherited their father's keen mental faculties. Abraham, the second child, grew to manhood, well educated, strong

69

Felix Mendelssohn-Bartholdy

willed, and steeped in Jewish tradition. With a natural bent for money matters, he launched into the financial world—first at Paris, then at Hamburg, and finally at Berlin.

When Abraham sought a "Sarah" from the tents of his father's people, he found her in the daughter of a Jewish family in Berlin. She was a young woman of culture, intelligence, and grace. Abraham won her heart, and after the wedding the now prosperous banker and his bride established themselves in Hamburg. Their first child, Fanny, was born, as the mother expressed, it, with "Bach fugue fingers." And then on November 3, 1809, the year that marked the passing of Haydn in Hungary, and the birth of Abraham Lincoln in far-off America, Jakob Ludwig Felix was born.

Frau Mendelssohn realized the importance of early molding the talents and character of her children. She gave them their first music lessons—beginning with five-minute doses. Fanny and Felix became increasingly devoted to each other, and to make music together was their joy of joys.

When the Mendelssohns were converted to Christianity they were baptized into the Lutheran faith. The addition of the Christian name Bartholdy helped to remove the stigma of their race, and became an open sesame to free society.

At ten Felix's remarkable talents had so developed that he made his first public appearance as a pianist. Once a week he sang at the Singakademie, where he appeared, as described by Devrient, in a "tight-fitting jacket, cut very low at the neck, over which the wide trousers were buttoned; into the slanting pockets of these the little fellow liked to thrust his hands, rocking his curly head from side to side, and shifting restlessly from one foot to the other."

Together with his music teacher Zelter, Felix, when twelve years old, journeyed to Weimar to visit Goethe. The sage and poet was acquainted with the teachings of Felix's grandfather and was as eager to see the young musician as Felix was to see the venerable poet.

The boy's sunny, unspoiled disposition, his lively, lisping

voice, and handsome bearing soon won the heart of Goethe. And his admiration turned to amazement on hearing his young guest improvise at the piano. Felix's remarkable ability to read at sight, and his storehouse of memorized pieces, including an arrangement of the *Chorale Symphony* of Beethoven, evoked the highest praise from Goethe. When Felix visited him a little later, the poet said, "I am Saul, and you are David. When I am sad and in low spirits you must come to me and calm me by your accords."

From his twelfth year onward Felix began to compose with regularity. Here again the environment and encouragement of his home nurtured the flowers of his creation. The Mendelssohn family, now consisting of four children, had moved to a suburb of Berlin. Sunday afternoon musicales were given regularly by members of the family circle and their guests. Works by the classic composers and new compositions of Felix were performed. Notables, including musicians such as Moscheles and Spohr, were among the visitors. Indeed, the home became a social mecca of Berlin. On one occasion the parents prevailed upon Moscheles, a noted pianist of the day, to give Felix lessons. After the first lesson the new teacher wrote in his diary, "I am quite aware that I am sitting next to a master, not a pupil."

Felix loved to travel. His parents realized, too, its importance as a part of his general education and as a background for his future work. So a trip was taken to Switzerland, enchanted land of lofty mountains, fertile valleys, and beautiful lakes. The boy was thus inspired to renewed activity in music, and doubtless his talent in painting found fresh impetus in the changing scenery afforded by this colossal garden.

The Mendelssohns had remodeled the buildings on the grounds of their palatial residence to take care of the music parties held there and to accomodate the host of friends who made this their favorite rendezvous. A choice group consisting of members whose ages were about the same as that of Felix met with frequent regularity and generally led in the spirited discussions. A paper called *The Garden Times* in summer and *Tea and*

Snow Times during the winter months, gave the various members of the group opportunity to express their own particular ideas along musical, literary, or philosophical lines.

In one issue Felix, a coeditor of the paper, contributed the following verses showing the reaction of his sensitive soul to the adverse criticism that some of his works had already received:

"If the artist gravely writes,
　To sleep it will beguile.
If the artist gaily writes,
　It is a vulgar style.

"If the artist writes at length,
　How sad his hearers' lot!
If the artist briefly writes,
　No one will care one jot.

"If an artist simply writes,
　A fool he's said to be.
If an artist deeply writes,
　He's mad; 'tis plain to see.

"In whatsoever way he writes
　He can't please every man.
Therefore let an artist write
　How he likes and can."

On an afternoon in the summer of 1826, Felix, with the "inner circle" of friends seated about him on the lawn, was reading a German translation of Shakespeare. Tragedies and comedies were discussed and cursorily dramatized by members of the circle. When *A Midsummer Night's Dream* was read, the youthful composer was so impressed that immediately he began visualizing it in a musical setting. During the days that followed, the music assumed definite shape and the overture to *A Midsummer Night's Dream* reached its finished form on August 6, 1826. This delightful music, and also the incidental music later written for the play, especially the scherzo, crystallize Mendelssohn's elegant and graceful style.

Felix's parents exercised sagacious care in their plans for his career. Money was no obstacle. Accordingly, a grand tour, to cover a period of several years, was arranged for him. The object of the journey was to "give him a knowledge of the world and form his character and manners."

In the spring of 1829 Felix boarded the *Attwood* for England. Three days later the small steamer, having met with rough seas and engine trouble, slowly plowed the last furrows of the Thames and docked at London. Felix was off to a bad start! There had been regurgitations within and without on the voyage, so that now his low spirits reflected the depth of the sea. However, the loving care of his friends, who met him, soon made him comfortable in the city, and he became his vivacious self again.

The London musical season was on. Felix made his debut as composer, conductor, and pianist with considerable success. He became the hub of the social whirl. Wherever he went a warm reception awaited him, with dinners and parties given in his honor. "It is fearful! It is maddening!" he wrote to his parents. "I am quite giddy and confused. London is the grandest and most complicated monster on the face of the earth."

The "conqueror" went on to new triumphs in Scotland. A visit was made to Fingal's Cave, in the Hebrides, an unusual cavern formed of basaltic columns, which was the haunt of seals and waterfowl. The impressions of its awesome beauty upon the composer became the actual inspiration for twenty bars of music which ultimately developed into the *Fingal's Cave* or *Hebrides* overture. His *Scotch Symphony in A minor,* written at a later date, also depicted the depth to which his soul was stirred by the exquisite scenes and lore of the highlands. "When God Himself takes to panorama painting," he wrote, "it turns out strangely beautiful."

Glasgow—Liverpool—northern Wales. At Coed-du, near Mold, Wales, Felix spent a number of days at the home of a friend, John Taylor, where the young composer endeared himself to the members of the family by his magnetic personality and refined manners. Together they visited points of interest, including the mines managed by his host. Home again in the evening, Felix improvised at the piano, recalling in tonal perspective the experiences they had had during the day.

The younger members of the family, in company with Felix, strolled through the garden to a favorite trysting place one afternoon. Their attention was drawn to a creeping vine with trumpet-shaped flowers. The youthful friends, ensconced on benches in a foliage-arbored recess, observed while Felix wrote out his "Scherzo in E minor" to show what the "fairies might play on these trumpets." Along the margin he traced a branch of the trumpet-flowered vine and dedicated the piece to one of the Taylor sisters. Original souvenir pieces were also given to each of the other sisters, but the little scherzo with the triple-tongue fanfare is the only one of his *Opus 16* that has remained popular through the years.

The capricious, elflike scherzo is particularly suitable to one aspect of Mendelssohn's style. This type of composition mirrors his bubbling, jovial nature and carefree life. Well-known examples are the "Rondo Capriccioso" for piano; the scherzo from *A Midsummer Night's Dream* for orchestra and the finale of his violin *Concerto in E minor,* which embodies the quintessence of delicacy and speed.

Interesting high lights of Mendelssohn's visit to the Taylor family were later written out in a letter by one of its members. An intimate glimpse of the young musician's serious as well as blithe character is seen in the following excerpts:

"Mr. Mendelssohn was not a bit 'sentimental,' though he had so much sentiment. Nobody enjoyed fun more than he, and his laughing was the most joyous that could be. One evening in hot summer we stayed in the wood above our house later than usual. We had been building a house of fir branches in Susan's garden up in the wood. We made a fire a little way off it, in a thicket among the trees—Mendelssohn helping with the utmost zeal, dragging up more and more wood. We tired ourselves with our merry work; we sat down round our fire, the smoke went off, the ashes were glowing, it began to get dark, but we did not like

to leave our bonfire. 'If we but had some music,' Mendelssohn
said 'could anyone get something to play?' Then my brother recol-
lected that we were near the gardener's cottages, and the gardener
had a fiddle. Off rushed our boys to get the fiddle. When it
came, it was the wretchedest [sic] thing in the world, and it had
but one string. Mendelssohn took the instrument into his hands
and fell into fits of laughter over it when he heard the sounds
it made. His laughter was very catching; he put us all into peals
of merriment. But he somehow afterwards brought beautiful
music out of the poor old fiddle, and we sat listening to one strain
after another till the darkness sent us home."

The letter continues rather intimately: "Sometimes he used
to talk very seriously with my mother. Seeing that we brothers
and sisters lived lovingly together and with our parents, he spoke
about this to my mother, told her how he had known families
where it was not so and used the words, 'You know not how happy
you are.'"

Shortly after returning to London, Felix hurt his knee when
the gig in which he was riding overturned. He was confined
to his bed for several months and his homeward journey delayed
until the latter part of November. Although obliged to use a
cane because of lameness, he was then able to take passage across
the channel and return to his family hearth. He spent the winter
at their Berlin residence and in May resumed his tour, this
time to Italy and Switzerland.

Among the versatile composer's several pursuits was that of
letter writing. His keen observation, his fine aesthetic sense, and
his descriptive powers are revealed in his letters no less than in
his compositions. After a day spent in the Alps he wrote:

"It was a day as if made on purpose. The sky was flecked with
white clouds floating far above the highest snow peaks, no mists
below on any of the mountains, and all their summits glittering
brightly in the morning air, every undulation and the face of
every hill clear and distinct. I remembered the mountains before only as huge peaks. It was their height that formerly took
possession of me. Now it was their boundless extent that I

particularly felt, their huge broad masses, the close connection of all these enormous fortresses, which seemed to be crowding together and stretching out their hands to each other. Then, too, recollect that every glacier, every snowy plateau, every rocky summit was dazzling with light and glory, and that the more distant summits of the further ranges seemed to stretch over and peer in upon us. I do believe that such are the thoughts of God Himself. Those who do not know Him may here find Him and the nature which He has created brought strongly before their eyes."

Then, when words became inadequate to express the grandeur of the natural beauties and of the treasures of art, his full emotions found release on wings of melody. At his bidding the play of the waters became cascades of music, the hills and valleys reverberated with the roll of the timpani, the majesty of the mountains rose in a crescendo of massive chords. Foremost among the works begun while he sojourned in Italy was the *Italian Symphony*.

As Mendelssohn pursued his varied interests and extensive travels, his eye was ever alert to the beautiful in the lives and works of others—and lo! in Frankfurt, the twenty-seven-year-old musician discovered what to him was a masterpiece of feminine pulchritude, a charming seventeen-year-old lass, Cecile Jeanrenaud. "Her serene and cheerful disposition," he wrote, "is like a cooling drink to my restless spirit."

The betrothal was soon announced, and on March 28, 1837, they were wed in the French Reformed church in Frankfurt. A simple, beautiful home life was established, and five curly-haired children came in turn to inspire the happy parents to new hymns of praise.

Religion and music, true and undefiled—the two greatest heavenly bodies to shed light on the way of earth's pilgrims—reached new heights of glory in Mendelssohn's several oratorios and cantatas. His first oratorio, *St. Paul*, was completed when the composer was twenty-six years of age. His *Hymn of Praise* was written to celebrate the four hundredth anniversary of the Gutenberg printing press, and was first given at a musical festival at Leipzig, in 1840, when a statue of the inventor was unveiled.

One day while reading the Scriptures, Mendelssohn came across the passage "Behold, the Lord passed by," and immediately confided to another musician in his company that this text suggested an oratorio. Subsequently, the picturesque figure of the prophet Elijah impressed him more and more as the ideal character around which the oratorio should center.

In 1845 actual writing of the score began, with the first part completed on May 23, 1846. In a letter to Jenny Lind, Mendelssohn wrote, "I am jumping about my room for joy. If it only turns out half as I fancy it is, how pleased I shall be!"

With the composer as conductor, the oratorio was given its first performance in Birmingham, England, on Wednesday, August 16, 1846. "The town hall was densely crowded, and it was observed that the sun burst forth as Mendelssohn took his place amid a deafening roar of applause from band, chorus, and audience."

In popularity second only to the *Messiah* by Handel, the *Elijah* continues to touch the hearts of men and women in all walks of life by its lofty, dramatic power. Through its medium the beauty of the story of one of the grand characters of Old Testament history is enhanced; the important spiritual lessons from his life are brought home to every listener with renewed emphasis.

Mendelssohn's keen dramatic sense and musical inspiration are jointly reflected throughout the oratorio in the fine association between the words and music. For instance, in three fine choruses of the prophets of Baal, there is depicted first, confidence, as they plead to their god to consume the sacrifice; then, intense religious fervor, as they cut themselves with lancets in order to awaken Baal; and finally, utter despair, as their prayers are unanswered, and the sacrifices lie unconsumed. In quiet contrast follows the simple prayer of faith from the lips of the prophet Elijah beginning, "Lord God of Abraham, Isaac, and of Israel, let it be known this day that Thou art God in Israel, and that I am Thy servant, and that I have done all these things at Thy word."

God delights, not in pomp and ceremony, nor in outward manifestations, as such, but in the simple sincere faith of the heart. He is neither coerced nor provoked by the babble of the throng, but is touched by the cry of even one weak and spiritually hungry soul.

With fidelity to the Scriptural narrative, Mendelssohn, by means of effective tonal colors, paints other events in the life of this man of God; his courage, as he appears in Ahab's court to announce a judgment from God; his mercy and faith in the healing of the widow's son; his human nature, as seen in his prayer, "It is enough," while resting, despondent, under the juniper tree. And withal, in the ever-changing experiences of his earthly career, this truth is made profoundly impressive— God watches over His servants.

Oratorios, such as the *Elijah,* as well as lesser works of similar quality, by combining Scriptural truth and the most sublime music, generate a singular power for good, and exert an influence in the direction of God's light and truth that is universally appealing.

Mendelssohn, a classic-romantic composer, had a deep respect for the forms and composers of the classical school, combined with a feeling for romantic and poetic expression. His style is particularly polished, though often lacking in depth and virility as compared with the styles of such composers as Beethoven and Schumann. It is generally conceded that because of his comparatively sunny, carefree life he was unable to plumb the depths of human emotion, and, as a result, his music is deficient in portraying certain phases of life. But his part in musical history is none the less significant, for even his musical moments of sheer joy, though ephemeral, are of the purest strain, and the elegance of his style is a model of lustrous finish.

Aside from his own creative contributions to musical literature, Mendelssohn further earned the gratitude of the world in his revival of the works of Bach. Nearly a century had gone since the passing of the Eisenach master, and his compositions had been all but forgotten. When Mendelssohn discovered these treasures of musical art he gave unstintingly of his time and talents toward their propagation and restoration. Many of Mendelssohn's compositions, too, bear unmistakable evidence of the influence of his classical prototype. There is an interesting point of analogy in that their most distinguished achievements were made in the same fields of composition; they set new standards of excellence in the organ and oratorio repertories.

The *Songs Without Words* of Mendelssohn, tone pictures serving to initiate the young musician into the works of better composers, are keys to his style, with the "Spring Song," the "Hunting Song," and the "Spinning Song" leading in popularity. His remarkable versatility is readily seen in the varied fields of composition—solo, orchestral, choral—in which he distinguished himself. His music expresses the strength and beauty of his personality; it is a diary of noble life dedicated to spreading the gospel of fine music.

Busy days—founding a great conservatory at Leipzig, conducting at the Gewandhaus concerts and elsewhere, composing, traveling, with eleven trips made to England alone—took their toll in vitiating the strength of the composer.

He returned home from his last trip to England, broken in health from overwork and burdened in spirit by the recent death of his sister Fanny. One of his last compositions, a little *Nachtlied* —"Departed Is the Light of Day"—seemed to presage his own passing. In his thirty-ninth year, at the height of his powers, the light of his life flared, flickered, and then went out; but the light of his deathless music lingers.

Frederic Francois Chopin

1809-1849

"Musical Poet"
"Musical Inventor"
"Musical Aristocrat"

PATRIOTISM is like the pulse of a nation. It stems from one of the strongest emotions that surge within the human breast. Men dare the jaws of death, bite at the heel of their oppressor, or passively waste away in prison, rather than surrender their allegiance to an alien power. True patriotism is more than a manifestation of loyalty to a particular homeland; it is, in its broader aspects, an expression of fidelity to principles of justice, equity, and freedom, as the foundation on which all sound and enduring governments rest. All down through the ages men have been moved to write some of history's most brilliant pages in vindication of these inherent human rights—in the stirring songs of poets, in the eloquent addresses of statesmen, and in deeds of valor on fields of battle. That country which recognizes the sovereignty of the individual becomes to its people a symbol of integrity and tolerance. It becomes, moreover, one of the sweetest harbingers that this earth affords of that land whose King rules in love.

The sons of Poland have shown, in outstanding degree, a patriotic zeal that has been unwavering in the face of years spent

6   81

Frederic Francois Chopin

in the balances, fluctuating between oppression and freedom. Her musician-sons, too, have shared this spirit in a large measure. Foremost among the names of her musician-patriots was that of Chopin. Patriotism affected his life; patriotism colored his creations. More recently, Paderewski, sometimes called Chopin II, showed a love for his country that was akin to a martyr's zeal. In the golden years of his career he sacrificed himself and his art for the cause of his country. When the goal was won he returned to his music with a new message—more serious, more profound. Again Poland's liberty was jeopardized, and finally crushed. Again Paderewski, then eighty, painfully, courageously concertized, though his music was but a shadow of that of his early years, in order by its proceeds to rekindle the lamp of hope in the hearts of Poland's sons.

When Poland was partitioned by Russia, Prussia, and Austria, between 1772 and 1795, the listening world heard rumblings of insurrection rise from the ravished land, and simultaneously voices, singing its pathetic minor strains; for even when repressed, the national feelings of the Poles burst forth in song. Subsequently, above the chorus a new voice was heard. Its message, couched in the language of tone, was profound and sensitive. It served not only to unite the Polish people but to arouse the world to the plight of this tragic land. It came from a gifted son who "voiced in music the very heart and soul of the Polish people."

Frederic Francois Chopin was born in Zelazowa-Wola, a short distance from Warsaw. "Polish villages are all alike," wrote Count Wodzinski in 1886, "a clump of trees surrounding the *dwor,* or nobleman's house; the barns, cow houses, and stables form a spacious square courtyard, in the middle of which a well has been sunk, to which the red-turbaned girls go to fill their pails; roads planted with poplars and fringed with thatched huts; then fields of rye and wheat, stirred by the wind as with rippling waves, gilded and gleaming in the sun; fields of yellow-blossomed colza, lucerne, and silvery clover; then forests which, in proportion as they are more or less remote, either stand out in dark masses against the horizon, or stretch out like a girdle of blue, or shimmer in a gauzy vapor. Such is Zelazowa-Wola." He goes on to tell of his visit to Chopin's birthplace: "A few feet away from the castle I paused in front of a little slate-roofed house, flanked with a small flight of wooden steps. . . . It is crossed by a gloomy vestibule. On the left, in a room lit by the ruddy flame of slowly burning logs, or by the flickering light of two candles placed one at each end of a long table, the serving maids spin as in olden days, relating to each other a thousand legends."

When Nicholas Chopin, Frederic's father, emigrated to Poland from France, he procured employment, first as a book-keeper in a tobacco firm, and later as a tutor in several homes of the aristocracy. It was at one of these homes that he met a titled young lady, who, although of the nobility, was not wealthy. They were married in 1806 and lived for several years in a cottage on the estate of a Count Skarbek. They were a fine couple with high principles and excellent abilities. Frederic, the second of four children, was the pet of his adoring sisters, Louise, Isabelle, and Emilienne. He was frail and pale-faced, and particularly sensitive to music, insomuch that on hearing it he often burst into tears. But he loved it dearly, especially piano music. At six he was given lessons from a Czech master, and at eight, played a concerto in a charity recital. "He was neither an intellectual prodigy nor a conceited puppy," wrote Niecks, his biographer, "but a naive, modest child, who played the piano as the birds sing, with unconscious art."

Even as a child, Frederic vacillated between sparkling vivacity and pensive dreaminess—traits that early crept into his music. He was a born actor and with his sisters took keen delight in writing and acting plays. Frederic's mimicry and impersona-tions were especially natural and real. His education was fairly thorough, not only in music, but in languages, mathematics, and other branches. Meanwhile, he imbibed his country's poetry and music, and thus the seeds were sown that would later burst forth and ripen in the sunlight of his maturity.

During his eleventh year Frederic composed a march for the Russian grand duke. While the little musician played it, the grand duke, otherwise stern, marched up and down the room in step with the music. It was hard to say who was more pleased —boy or duke. Frederic then improvised. As he did so, he, as was his habit, raised his eyes upward. "Why do you always look upward, little one?" asked the duke "Can you see notes up there?" Ah, yes! Young as he was, Frederic may have been dreaming of the day when his notes would soar into the blue, as free as birds, symbols of freedom and peace in his beloved Poland.

Frederic's first opus, the *Rondo in C minor*, was written when he was fifteen, and a pupil of the conservatory. After he graduated from the lyceum at the age of seventeen, his education was furthered by visits to important centers, such as Berlin and Dresden. New social contacts, changing scenery, and the praise of critics proved exhilarating to the young genius. Nevertheless, nostalgia would have taken possession of him had it not been for the friendship of his piano. He wrote a friend at Warsaw: "I feel so lonely and neglected here, I cannot live as I would like. I must dress, must appear in the salons with cheerful face; but when I am in my room again, I have a confidential talk with my piano and tell it all my woes, as to my best friend here in Vienna."

Back again in Warsaw, his days were busy completing important compositions begun on his travels. He also gave several concerts, with warm public response. These mundane affairs were taken in fine fettle, but there was an affair of the heart that made the emotional teeterboard of the romantic dreamer sway rather violently again, and only the balm of music and hard work brought the jilted swain back to his senses. Simultaneously, a national revolt against Russian oppression was brewing in the land. This further battered his bruised spirit, and although he would have favored staying in Poland to bear arms for his country, it was thought best, in view of his frail health, that he leave for a more pacific environment. So arrangements were completed for him to journey to Paris and then to London. But he was leaving with great reluctance. In a letter to a friend he poured out his feelings: "I still have a presentiment that I am leaving

Warsaw never to return. I bear within me the conviction that I am saying farewell to my country forever. Ah! How sad it must be to die anywhere but in one's birthplace." At a farewell banquet given in his honor, he received a silver goblet filled with Polish soil—a tender reminder that he kept until his death.

When Frederic reached Paris in 1831, it was high noon on the timepiece of romanticism. Brilliant, original thinkers, such as Hugo, Dumas, and a host of other lights were appearing in the literary firmament. Likewise, in the field of music, important figures such as Meyerbeer and Rossini in opera; Liszt, the incomparable virtuoso and teacher, and others, were making their names. Then later Chopin was to meet Schumann and Mendelssohn, prominent exponents of the romantic movement.

The youthful Chopin had been in Paris but a few days when the great and near great in the world of letters and art began making a path to his door, for news of this remarkable Polish lad and of his coming to Paris had preceded him. Berlioz and Legouve were among the early callers. "We ascended to the second floor of a little lodging house," Legouve wrote, "and I found myself face to face with a pale, melancholy, elegant young man with a slight foreign accent, brown eyes of incomparable softness and limpidity, chestnut hair almost as long as that of Berlioz and falling in a wisp on his brow. . . . His person, his playing, and his works were in such harmony that it seemed as if they could no more be separated than the different features of the same face. The tone so peculiarly his own, which he drew from the piano, was like the glance of his eye; the somewhat morbid delicacy of his nature was akin to the poetic melancholy of his nocturnes; and the care and choiceness with which he dressed enabled one to understand the almost modish elegance of certain parts of his works."

So Chopin stood at the crossroads. Twenty odd years of his life had been spent; he had lived in a "sweet home" of love and tranquillity; had associated with the aristocracy as well as with peasants; had breathed the spirit of Poland in its poetry, dance music, and folklore; had partaken with a relish of the fruits offered by the works of the old masters of music. Thereby he had learned to *live*. And now he was to relive in his music the impressions of his youth. He found himself at the entrance to a new world.

Nearly twenty years lay ahead. In creative originality, in realization of his musical dreams, they were to be years of plenty; in health and in the pursuit of the joy of living they were to be lean years. He would not feel want as did Mozart and Schubert, but he would suffer. He would frequently fall in love and as quickly fall out again. He would taste of life's bitter waters. But out of the bitter would come sweet music.

Unlike those of many of the composers whose earlier works often imitate the masters with whom they are apprenticed, Chopin's works, including his earliest, were marked by originality. Even the nocturnes, which were patterned after those of John Field, are so superior in concept as to far outshine those of his Irish predecessor. In the nocturnes, Chopin's dreamy, melancholy, sometimes morbid nature finds an ideal vehicle of expression. "Chopin loved the night and its starry mysteries," wrote Huneker; "his nocturnes are true night pieces, some wearing an agitated remorseful countenance; others seen in profile only; while many are like whisperings at dusk."

A particularly enchanting feature of Chopin's nocturnes is his use of delicate *fioriture* to adorn the melody, like a blanket of gossamer lace, covering with feathery lightness these melodies of the night. Another innovation, peculiar to Chopin's works was his use of the *tempo rubato*. Liszt, who had heard Chopin play, describes its effect as follows: "An irregularly interrupted movement, subtle, broken and languishing, at the same time flickering like a flame in the wind, undulating like the surface of a wheat field, like treetops moved by a breeze." The *Nocturne in E-flat major, Opus 9, Number 2,* has, among all the nocturnes, won the widest circle of friends, with the *Nocturne in F-sharp major* second in popularity.

During these years it was customary for the elite of the literary and musical residents of Paris to meet frequently in social "get-togethers." Celebrities, such as Liszt, Mendelssohn, Rossini, and Chopin, contributed their share of wit and repartee on these occasions. Sparks of humor and satire flew from the tongues of budding and mature geniuses; often as not, the sparks left a sting. Musical improvisation was in order. On one such occasion, the story is told, after a violinist had received a warm reception to his fine performance of an original work, Chopin, who was present, overheard one of the ladies remark, "What a pity that the piano is incapable of these effects! It is brilliant, dramatic, resourceful, what you will; but only the violin can stir the heart in that way." "Chopin rose," relates Edward Perry, brilliant blind pupil of Liszt, "bowing with one of his equivocal smiles, half sad, half playfully mocking, and improvised this *Nocturne in D-flat major, Opus 27, Number 2,* a perfect reproduction of all the best violin effects, a *cantilena* and all, including the double-stopping in the second theme, with a certain warmth and poetry added which were his own." The seed here sown later matured into the beautiful nocturne loved and played by pianists and violinists alike.

Chopin's *Berceuse* is one of the earliest examples of "impressionistic" music, later to be developed by men such as Ravel, Debussy, and Stravinsky. The seventy measures of this cradle song are built on an accompaniment of three simple chords, and throughout almost the entire piece an undulating figure based on the tonic and dominant seventh chords recurs with monotonous regularity in the left-hand part, reminding one of the rocking cradle. Meanwhile, an exquisitely tender melody begins in the third measure, lasting only four measures, then reappears throughout the piece disguised in constantly changing variations. It is as though the mother, while repeatedly singing the simple cradle song, previews, in her mind, her child's growth during months to come, and pictures the object of her love, dressed in the pretty costumes she has already prepared. Paradoxically, the two most famous cradle songs, the *Berceuse* of Chopin and the *Cradle Song* of Brahms, were written by bachelors.

The rhythmic and emotional elements of dance forms, such

as the waltz, the mazurka, and the polonaise received fresh impetus and exhaustive treatment in Chopin's hands. While his waltzes are essentially French in style, the mazurka and the polonaise are of Polish origin. The mazurkas originated with the Mazurian peasants, and mingle love and patriotism. The polonaise originated at the coronation of the French prince, Henri d'Anjou, as king of Poland, in the latter part of the sixteenth century. At the reception following the coronation a long procession of notables of the court wound past the throne to the stately strains of the polonaise. Thus the polonaise has more of chivalry and pomp than does the mazurka. Chopin's *Military Polonaise,* while not the greatest of his polonaises, is the best known.

One of the most remarkable sets of pieces from the pen of Chopin was given the prosaic title *Etudes,* or *Studies.* While they are studies in technique and interpretation, they are neither commonplace nor dry, but masterpieces of rare beauty and emotional significance. The composer referred to the beautiful melody of *Opus 10, Number* 3 as one of the finest melodies he had ever written, and on hearing one of his pupils play this etude, exclaimed, "Oh, my country!" The *Revolutionary Etude,* it is said, was written after the composer, on his way to Paris, heard of the capitulation of Warsaw in 1831. The very difficult *Etude in Thirds, Opus 25, Number 6* acts like an exhilarating tonic on its listeners. Apropos of this charm is an almost incredible story regarding this etude told by Paderewski in his memoirs:

"One day I was practicing in my little room in Vienna. Among the pieces I was then studying, and which I had to play every day as a finger exercise, was a certain study by Chopin, a study in thirds. I was just starting to work—I lit the candles and sat down at the piano. The room was very dark, you know; there were so many tall shrubs growing close to the window. Then, suddenly in the midst of my playing, there came down from the ceiling right onto the piano desk, something like a tiny silver thread. It attracted my attention and I looked a little closer, and then I saw—a spider attached to it. He hung there motionless and appeared to be listening to my playing, and as long as I played the particular study in *thirds,* the little spider remained there perfectly still on his line.

"And now comes the interesting thing. After finishing the study in thirds, I went on to another study—in sixths this time, and the moment I began it, the spider turned himself quickly about and hurried up to the ceiling. Well, it struck me at the moment as very funny, and I was interested and deeply intrigued. I said to myself, 'Now, I must see whether that spider is really musical or not—whether he meant to come down to listen on purpose, or by accident.' So I suddenly stopped my study in *sixths* and quickly started again the one in *thirds.* Instantly, down came the little spider! He seemed to slide down his line, and this time to the very end, and sat on the piano desk and listened! He did not seem at all frightened—only deeply interested in the music.

"He had aroused my interest greatly, and I wondered if he would appear the next morning. I was very curious about him— I felt sure I should see him again. Well, he did appear the moment I began my day's work with the thirds. That little thread still hung from the ceiling, and down he came the moment I touched the piano, and this same thing continued all that day, and the next day; and for many weeks he came—he was a faithful companion. Whenever I started the study in thirds, the little spider came quickly to the piano desk and listened. After a time I arrived so far as to be able to see his eyes—so brilliant, like tiny, shining diamonds. He would sit immovable, or hang immovable I should say, during that Chopin *Etude,* perfectly content and perfectly quiet. But the moment I stopped that particular study, back he went quickly to the ceiling and disappeared."

A weak condition of the lungs seemed to run in the Chopin family. The composer developed rather alarming symptoms in 1836. Thinking that a change of climate would improve his health, Chopin and a group of friends, including George Sand, the French novelist, left for Majorca in October, 1838. The islands of Majorca and Minorca lie in the Mediterranean—

east of Spain. The tourists had some difficulty finding suitable living quarters, and finally decided on the shelter of a wing of an old monastery called Valdemosa. "It was an old ruined building of Gothic masonry, with hollow, stone corridors and silent cells overlooking a cypress-laden cemetery."

Soon the cloistered walls resounded with the strains of exotic music. The cells, no longer silent, became the cradles of new-born melodies. For it was here the master wrote most of his preludes and perfected those already begun. "Gleanings from his portfolio," these gems intermingle the strong emotions that welled in the heart of the suffering genius. George Sand, who was near or present when the preludes were composed, wrote: "Many of them call up to the mind's eye visions of dead monks and the sound of their funeral chants which obsessed him; others are suave and melancholy; these would come to him in his hours of sunshine and health, amid the sound of children's laughter beneath his window, the distant thrum of the guitar, and the song of birds among the damp leafage, or at the sight of the pale little roses blooming above the snow. Others again are dreary and sad, and wring the heart while charming the ear."

Meanwhile, the wet seasonal weather, together with insufficient nourishing food, because of the suspicious attitude of the native traders, brought a relapse to the composer. When he failed to improve, a consultation of doctors was held. "One said I would die," stated Chopin in a letter; "the second said I was about to die; and the third said I was already dead." When he failed to rally in the mild Majorca climate, it was decided that the company should return to France at the first change to better weather. The suspicious natives felt relieved when they were rid of the sickly visitor.

Outside of visits to England and Scotland, the remainder of Chopin's days were spent in France. He became steadily weaker, but in creative achievement increasingly greater: Ballades, scherzos, sonatas, the *Fantasie in F minor*—all are marked by epic utterances, and reveal the mature Chopin.

As Chopin neared the close of his second twenty years, his

immaculately attired, lean figure could hardly cast a shadow. His impaired breathing became heavier, his steps tottering, until he was unable to leave his bed. When he knew the end was near he asked one of his bedside guests, a Countess Potacka, to sing for him. During the night he breathed the final cadence of his own life's song. The silver goblet of Polish soil, given to the composer twenty years earlier, was emptied over the casket. His body was buried in Paris, but his heart was returned to Poland.

Chopin, sometimes called the Tennyson, sometimes the Poe, of music, had resolved "to create a new art era," and this he verily realized in his new "means of expression" and in his new approach to the resources of the piano. He was a music-specialist. "He came not," wrote Schumann, "with an orchestral army, as great geniuses are wont to come. He possesses only a little cohort, but it belongs to him wholly and entirely, even to the last hero."

Though his realm was small, he spoke in a universal tongue. He spoke, moreover, from his heart, revealing meanwhile the "soul" of his beloved instrument. He addresses himself to everyone. His voice, having leaped across the boundaries of his native country, appeals to all, great and low, each to do his share to perpetuate liberty—of men and of nations.

Robert Alexander Schumann

1810-1856

*"Thou didst rule with a golden scepter
over a splendid world of tones ..."*

～♪～

CLASSICAL music, in a general sense, is the "survival of the fittest"; it represents the best and most original thinking in music regardless of time or school. More specifically, it refers to styles developed during a certain period of modern history, as contrasted with those of romanticism which immediately followed. In style, classical music is pure music, music for its own sake; romantic music, on the other hand, is personal. Classicism stresses the *letter*, romanticism the *spirit*. Classicism chisels in cold marble; romanticism imparts the blush of life. In the transition from classicism to romanticism, the fine lines from the pencil-point brushes of Mozart broaden and deepen until the heart of romanticism is reached in the flaming colors of passion and tragedy of Schumann.

Robert Schumann was born in an atmosphere of books, and doubtless his poetic and literary bent was given its first stimulus as he browsed through the musty shelves of his father's bookshop in the little town of Zwickau in Saxony. He came to revel in the verses of Goethe and Schiller, and to worship the heroes of Jean Paul Richter.

93

Robert Alexander Schumann

Four boys and a girl made up the happy, affectionate Schumann family. When Robert was seven, he received music lessons of an indifferent sort from a self-taught organist of the town, and thus became acquainted with the masters—Haydn, Mozart, and Beethoven. In a short time he was able to improvise at the piano, and delighted in picturing the characters of his friends in his playing. Sometimes he would place these impressions on paper, either in the form of music or in the form of poetry.

Robert's thorough academic education was begun at the Zwickau Gymnasium when he was but ten. Along with his studies he found time for his music; he formed an orchestra, developed his knowledge of the music of the great masters, and composed chorals.

When Herr Schumann died, the sixteen-year-old Robert was deprived of a kindly hand to guide his increasingly melancholy and taciturn nature. Frau Schumann appreciated Robert's poetical and musical inclinations, but did not look with favor on a career for him in these fields. She seemed to think that the profession of law would furnish her son a more secure means of livelihood than would the arts.

Robert acquiesced in his mother's judgment and entered the University of Leipzig when he was eighteen, with the express purpose of specializing in law. But it was with a feeling of frustration that he pursued the various courses; he was out of his element, and found it difficult to rationalize his inner feelings. He managed to procure a piano, and spent several hours each day in practice, during which the sunshine of music burst through the clouds of his disappointment. Then he heard about a music teacher in Leipzig who was one of the best in Germany at the time. He did not wait long before he arranged to meet this professor, Frederick Wieck, a great, mean man, who was to figure largely in Robert's life, as the source of both joy and sorrow.

As Robert pursued his studies, the door to beautiful music opened wider, and he gazed on green fields of natural expression, unplucked fruits from the groves of his own planting, and, on the horizon, a golden sunset bathed a rich harvest of imagination and achievement. Meanwhile, the door to jurisprudence, repellent to his type of personality, was heavily closing.

Robert knew, however, that before he could launch out on a musical career, he must, dutiful son that he was, gain his mother's consent. "My whole life," he wrote as he pleaded with his mother on July 30, 1830, "has been a struggle between poetry and prose, between music and law. Practical life seems to me to be an ideal as lofty as art. . . . But what prospects are open in Saxony to one who is not of noble birth, who has neither high influence nor fortune, and has no real love for beggarly legal practice and two-penny-half-penny squabbles? . . . Now I am at the crossroads and shrink in alarm at the question: Which way am I to turn? If I follow my inward monitor, it points to the path of art, and I believe that is the right path. . . . There is no more torturing thought for a man than that of an unhappy and sterile future which he has prepared for himself." He closed the letter by requesting that the decision of his career be left with his teacher, Wieck.

Fortunately, Frau Schumann accepted her son's suggestion to abide by the decision of his professor, and erelong the youth was in an ecstasy of joy when he received his mother's consent that he follow music seriously and the further word that she had added her blessing. "Music is your faithful mistress," she wrote, "your faithful friend in suffering and joy. What gentle, soothing consolation is given us by music! Be true to her, then, since you have chosen her as the companion of your earthly pilgrimage!"

Robert realized that even twenty was rather late in the day, with his haphazard background in musical training, to prepare for a pianistic career. So he made use of every minute, often practicing on a silent keyboard while riding in a carriage. Then the idea of a short cut to Parnassus struck him: He would mechanically suspend the unwieldly fourth finger while practicing with the others. But unfortunately—or *fortunately*—the device permanently lamed not only this finger but the entire right hand. His career as a pianist was ended. He must leave the byway of *reproduction*. But ahead stretched the highway of *musical creation*.

Perhaps his visits to his teacher would necessarily have ended with this sudden turn of events, but Wieck had a daughter—as lovely as her father was unlovely. She was a musician in her own right and was to become one of the greatest pianists the world has known. Robert loved Clara and she loved him. He was determined that someday he would win her hand. Herr Wieck, however, was as determined that he would not. To think that his talented daughter, already established as a successful pianist, should marry an obscure, poor student! No, indeed!

There was no trifling with father Wieck. His churlishness had driven his wife from their home. Now his temerity had reached the stage that he would resort to anything, regardless of how base, to separate Clara from her lover. At times Robert thought he had the "rose" within his grasp, when an avalanche of verbal blows from Wieck sent him sprawling again. Clara pleaded for her father's blessing on their friendship—but in vain. After an enforced separation the lovers met at a concert during which Clara played Robert's *Sonata in F-sharp minor.* "Did you not understand," she wrote later, "that I played it because I knew no other way of showing you a little of what was going on within me? I might not do it in secret, so I did it in public. Do you think my heart was not trembling?"

When Robert and his beloved decided they had borne Wieck's insolence long enough, they realized that their only recourse was to take the matter to court. Wieck fought to the bitter end, but was finally silenced by the action of the court; and only then were Robert and Clara free to plan their lives, together—unmolested.

The struggle had been bitter and long, but it was not without its bright side. The quest for his hard-earned "prize" had called forth the best that was in him, and inspired him to write some of his noblest works. In the roles of his beloved, his betrothed, and later as his wife, Clara touched the hidden fountains of his mind. His *Phantasiestucke, Kreisleriana, Sonata in F-sharp minor,* the *Scenes From Childhood,* and six books of *Lieder* (songs) were inspired by, or dedicated to, her.

7

Schumann was a man of versatile genius. He possessed a rare literary talent. His faculty to weigh accurately the merits of contemporary musicians and their works has been confirmed in history's pages. As early as 1833 Schumann conceived the idea of a musical review on a different plane from those already extant. The purpose of *Die Neue Zeitschrift fur Musik* was to champion the cause of serious music, to herald the rise of new talents, to exalt the great masters in a new light, and to flout the "standpatters," and the charlatans in art. He drew about him a following of supporters and likewise an imaginative circle of musicians, who under the fancied leadership of King David, musician and poet of Israel, should go forth to do battle against the Philistines (enemies of romanticism)—that band opposed to advancement into new light and beauty. Not a few of Schumann's musician-friends had their counterparts in the Davidsband. The last number of the *Carnaval,* the "March of the Hosts of David Against the Philistines," was a veritable battle hymn for these "music crusaders."

Schumann often wrote under the pseudonyms Florestan and Eusebius; Florestan representing the aggressive, bold side of his nature, and Eusebius the introspective and tender side. Schumann's compositions, too, often adopt these two contrasting styles. In his *Kreisleriana* moments of fiery aspiration alternate with those of tender repose. Similar contrasts abound throughout the *Fantasy Pieces (Opus 12).* In *Soaring* the aspiring Florestan side of the composer's personality rises above the obstacles that beset the paths of life to new heights of achievement. In the little tone poem "Why?" Eusebius pleads for an answer to thwarted hopes. It was written during the time Schumann's efforts to win Clara Wieck were rebuffed by her father. It is a missive in tonal language, written in a moment of disillusionment and addressed to his ladylove. With a sense of futility over the long-drawn-out struggle to break the barriers, made by her father, to their marriage, simply, imploringly, he pleads: Why?

The romantic composers and poets alike produced some of their most tender musings in response to the peace of nature at evening. Chopin composed a complete album of nocturnes; Schumann wrote his *Evening* and his night pieces. The "Nacht-stuck in F," more familiarly known as the "Hymn Tune, Canon-bury," recalls the spirit of Byron's lines:

> "It is the hour when from the boughs
> The nightingale's high note is heard;
> It is the hour when lovers' vows
> Seem sweet in every whispered word,
> And gentle winds and waters near
> Make music to the listening ear.
> Each flower the dews have lightly wet,
> And in the sky the stars are met,
> And on the wave is deeper blue,
> And on the leaf a browner hue;
> And in the heaven that clear obscure,
> So softly dark and darkly pure,
> Which follows the decline of day,
> As twilight melts beneath the moon away."

Many of the greatest creations of poets, painters, and composers have had their inspiration in scenes and moods of nature. The psalmist recognized a music of the spheres when he wrote, "The heavens declare the glory of God." There are the deep organ tones of the great ocean, the roll of the timpani in the thunder, the aeolian harp in the branches of a pine forest touched by a zephyr breeze, the chimes from dripping water in earth's caverns, the voices of insects and animals and birds. So all nature expresses itself—culminating in a grand cosmic symphony. The composer enters this huge garden of tone, and capturing a mood from the palette of life's experiences, opens to mankind a vista of new colors and scenes.

> "There's music in all things if men had ears;
> The earth is but an echo of the spheres."

Schumann's "Prophet Bird," the most popular of his *Forest Scenes,* is a mystical miniature in tonal colors. This impressionistic allusion to nature goes beyond the imitation of the song of a bird and gives the song a subtle meaning, wherein the bird senses lurking dangers, or instinctively prophesies, in varied calls, of coming changes of weather. Its style is suggestive of the idioms of some modern composers.

The same subtlety characterizes most of Schumann's works. His music runs deep. For that reason his music was not first appreciated, and only time has fathomed its depth and proved its worth. "Schumann's music appeals to contemplative souls and deep minds," wrote Liszt, "who are not content to remain on the surface of things, but know how to plunge into deep waters to seek the hidden pearl."

Schumann's tendency to frequent changes of mood is reflected in several sets of pieces from his pen. His *Kreisleriana, Papillons,* and the *Carnaval* are mood-mosaics, suggested by incidents and friendships of his life. In larger forms his contributions to music literature include sonatas, the ever-delightful *Piano Concerto in A minor,* the *Quintet for Pianoforte and Strings,* five symphonies, including the *Spring and Rhenish,* trios, and quartets. He wrote a cantata, *Paradise and Peri,* and several operas, notably *Faust* and *Manfred.* His art songs are among the greatest in song literature. *The Scenes From Childhood* and the *Album for the Young* gave expression to his lighter moods. They were composed in moments of relaxation, and they bring to the hearer's mind a picture of the master, seated by his fireside, and surrounded by his children, recalling tales and pranks and scenes of his own childhood. Two of the most famous of all the poet-composer's works, "The Happy Farmer" and "Traumerei" (Dreaming), are found in these albums.

Schumann aimed at an ideal in his music and literary essays rather than popular favor. His style of composition is individual, with new rhythms, fuller chordal texture, polyphonic meanders, and deep poetic feeling, as marked features. These nuggets of original musical and literary thought have been a source of inspiration to many aspiring musicians and music lovers. One maxim, gleaned from nearly seventy similar ones addressed to younger musicians, will suffice here to indicate the lofty trend of his idealism: "Play nothing as you grow older, which is merely *fashionable*. Time is precious. One must have a hundred lives if he would acquaint himself only with all that is good."

In Schumann's maxim lies the positive solution to music of a questionable nature. As appreciation for better music develops, the desire for cheap and shallow music melts away as dew in the sunlight. By constant association with wholesome music, even children acquire a natural love for it, and, simultaneously, an antipathy toward music that is trivial or degrading.

There is an obvious danger in indulging in the Tin Pan Alley type of music; there is a more subtle danger in a failure to demarcate between the truly noble music and the meaningless, sensuous music that so often reaches our homes and even passes through the portals of many churches. Music should not be selected merely because it is free from evil. It should be chosen, over and beyond this, to appropriate Ruskin's principle of judging the merits of a literary work, for its "possession of good."

Above all others, the people proclaiming the message of the third angel should, most surely, have a distinctive *message* in their music. In order that the ministry of the Word and the ministry of music may collaborate effectively to the glory of God and the uplift of men, it is necessary that the music's sanctity, purity, and deeper emotional appeal be maintained.

The wide range of selections within the realm of fine religious and secular musical literature is so varied that the tastes of any and all ranks of listeners, from the lowliest to the most erudite, may there find keen enjoyment and receive therefrom a rich reward. The novice in music will, perhaps, reject Brahms' *Second Symphony*, but is likely thoroughly to enjoy the same composer's *Hungarian Dances*. He may be bored with the polyphonic labyrinths of a Bach fugue, but be charmed by the piquant orchestration and quaint rhythms of Tchaikovsky's *Nutcracker Suite*. As each musical pilgrim finds his particular level of appreciation—if he is determined that his sense of the beautiful shall not remain static, and if he is willing to face the light of musical opportunity and to grow in "musical grace"—he will find himself on the path to a deeper emotional and spiritual experience. He will come to "accept music as a gift, a precious gift from God." He will be constrained to travel on to the Celestial City, where the redeemed of earth shall hear music "in all its glory and beauty."

For fourteen years the Schumanns lived a happy, busy life together. Madame Schumann, besides her other duties, spent considerable time in concertizing. Her husband accompanied her to other countries such as Russia and Holland, where they were royally received. He often spoke of the blessing of his life in having a "wife to whom I am bound by art, mental affinity, the habit of many years' friendship, and the deepest, holiest love. . . . My life is filled with joy and activity." He devoted most of his time to composition. Other duties included teaching in Mendelssohn's conservatory at Leipzig and the position of city music director at Dusseldorf.

In the midst of all these activities a shadow that had been lurking near the Schumann household for some years, crossed its threshold never to depart. The master felt its presence when he wrote to a friend, "Music is silent. . . . Night is beginning to fall." For two years hallucinations clouded the course of his mind.

His derelict ship had settled in the doldrums. His mariner's compass and sextant had been impaired in the severe gales which his life-ship had weathered. Alone, as its captain, he paced the deck, miserable in his chains—alone, yet not alone, for near at hand Clara Schumann waited, seeking in every way to ease his suffering and to pilot their course. A gentle breeze brought lucid moments. But as they neared the land, what had appeared to be the beginning of new hope and security proved to be a mirage. It was, rather the end of his way.

Clara Schumann returned to comfort her family of seven children. Then, gathering her garments of talent and courage about her, she went forth alone to show the world—through her matchless playing—the charts of her illustrious husband's earlier voyages to strange lands of music and his treasure-troves gathered from beyond the seas.

Franz Liszt

1811-1886

The Greatheart of Music

A GYPSY caravan, winding across the western Hungarian plain, came to a halt at the outskirts of the little peasant village of Raiding. Children, chattering in monkey fashion; women, young and old, decked in gaily colored dresses; large dogs, lop-eared and dirty—all seemed to tumble out of the covered wagons at one time. The horses were unhitched and allowed to graze near by, while the men, with the ease that comes of much practice, quickly set up camp.

As the villagers and country folk gathered around the camp in the evening, the gypsies presented their customary show by the light of a huge bonfire and torches. The women sang and danced and told fortunes. The men accompanied on their cymbals and violins.

One little boy, squatting in the front row of onlookers, watched, wide-eyed. He glanced from fiddler to dancer and back to fiddler again. The haunting melodies and syncopated rhythms held him spellbound. Someday that handsome, blue-eyed boy would, in fancy, rekindle these gypsy fires and bring the gypsy airs to flower in his own rhapsodic music. Franz was one of the last to leave as the dances ceased and the fires burned low.

103

Franz Liszt

Franz's father, Adam Liszt, was a superintendent on the estate of Prince Esterhazy. He held his position not by choice but from necessity. He had wished to become a professional musician, but had had to abandon his dream for the more certain income of his present position. But he spent his leisure time in playing the piano and violin, and in dreaming of musical conquests in the land of "might-have-been."

The first inkling of Franz's precocious musical memory came, when, one evening, the Liszts heard their six-year-old son singing, with remarkable accuracy, themes from a piano concerto, played earlier in the afternoon by his father. Adam Liszt lost no time in giving Franz lessons, and the puny, delicate lad learned with uncanny ease. His hearing was unusually accurate; his fingers were so nimble they seemed to be made for the piano; and best of all, he loved his music—just loved it! A new light came to the eyes of Adam Liszt. It seemed certain now that in Franz his dreams would come true.

Franz's progress was so rapid that by the time he was nine he was able to appear in several recitals with excellent success. News of the wonder-lad reached the palace of Prince Esterhazy. It required very little urging on the part of proud Papa Liszt to have the prince arrange for a concert in the drawing room of the palace. Franz was not in the least perturbed by the many royal dignitaries that made up his audience that evening. That he was handsome, with his heavy blond hair and slender, erect carriage, was soon forgotten as he filled the salon with music's "perfumes." His fine interpretations and improvisations proved so promising that, at the close of the concert, a subscription was raised which would give him a musical education.

Franz was now on the road toward mastery of the piano. Papa Liszt knew, as plans were laid for his son's future, that he who aspires to become the master of a worthy instrument must first become its slave. He decided on Vienna as the first choice of cities offering the best music-laden atmosphere for the lad. He decided on Czerny, one of the "three C's" of music, and a Beethoven pupil, as the most desirable teacher,

In high spirits Franz, together with his father and mother, left their little village for the city of their dreams. They sought out Czerny, and Franz was given an audition. The professor had written a mass of studies for developing piano technique (to the dismay of piano students ever since). He was, moreover, a stickler for details, but Franz's fresh and promising performance set him too to dreaming. "You may become a greater pianist than any of us," was his verdict. Franz progressed so rapidly under his guidance that Czerny declined a fee for the lessons, saying that the pupil's progress was sufficient remuneration.

Many months of diligent practice followed, and then it was decided that Franz was ready to make his Viennese debut. The eleven-year-old prodigy had made great strides in his playing, and the close of the concert found him bowing with childish nonchalance to the thunderous applause. Amid this ovation, the story goes, Beethoven, who was in the audience, stepped onto the platform, embraced Franz, and kissed him on the forehead. To Franz this was the sweetest acclaim that could come his way.

This triumph served to widen Papa Liszt's horizon. Ah, there was Paris! And the Conservatory! What an opportunity for Franz. So they left Vienna for the French capital. Arrangements for suitable living quarters were made as soon as they arrived in the city, and plans were laid for visiting the Conservatory the following day. When, with high hopes, they reached the exclusive music school, they were ushered into the office of the director, Cherubini. But Cherubini was an austere fellow, with definite ideas about adhering to regulations, including the one that only nationals would be permitted to attend the school. No amount of begging would alter his decisions, and so the Liszts, crestfallen, slowly left the building. They felt that a precious link in their plans for the boy's future success had been lost.

But success may be met just as surely on a bypath as on the highroad of life. When the Lizsts found one road closed they chose another. As soon as it was rumored about the musical circles that the.Hungarian boy-marvel was in the capital, he was invited to play at important gatherings in the city. His appearances excited the greatest wonder in his audiences, and as a result, a third capital, London, made a bid to see the budding genius. The "little Liszt," as he was called, played before George IV and other important English personages, astonishing his hearers wherever he played.

Fortunately Franz did not lose his equilibrium over the adoration and pampering that came his way. As he grew older he came to resent this treatment more and more. He often said, "I would rather be anything in the world than a musician in the pay of great folk, patronized and paid by them like a conjurer or a clever dog." Neither did he rest on his laurels. When he was thirteen he had already composed an opera. The family returned to Paris, then back to England for more concerts, and finally another tour, this time to Switzerland.

The Liszts were busy. They seemed to be running a race with time, and winning. But they had failed to reckon with the limitations of the flesh. Franz became exhausted first, but a complete rest brought him to full health again. Then his father became suddenly ill, and died.

Madame Liszt and Franz, then in his seventeenth year, rented a small apartment in Paris, and the youth settled down to giving lessons. The next several years found him successfully engaged in teaching, until he lost his heart to a pupil-lassie near his own age. It mattered not to them that she was the daughter of a wealthy count while he was the son of a steward. The lessons became longer, the music more romantic, discipline less exacting. Then, like a lightning flash from the blue, the count curtly dismissed the young teacher with orders that he should not return.

Franz's dream castle had collapsed. He became as one lost. He wanted to renounce the world and enter the priesthood. Even his music was laid aside. He lingered in this state of apathy for many, many months.

Then two things happened to his young life that removed the scales from his eyes: he became fired by the spirit of the French Revolution of 1830, with all its implications in art and music, and by the playing of that master of the violin, Paganini. When he heard the great Italian violinist in concert, he decided to emulate his mastery, and to do at the piano what he was doing with the violin. From that day forward, inspiration and drudgery clasped hands and made of Franz Liszt one of the greatest pianists the world has known.

"My mind and my fingers are working like two lost souls," he wrote to one of his pupils. "Homer, the Bible, Plato, . . . Beethoven, Bach, . . . are all about me. I study them, meditate on them, devour them furiously. In addition, I work four or five hours at exercises, thirds, sixths, octaves, tremolos, repeated notes, cadenzas, etc. . . . 'I, too, am a painter!' exclaimed Michelangelo, the first time he saw·a masterpiece. . . . Though small and poor, your friend has never ceased to repeat these words of that great man since Paganini's last concert." One of his biographers, speaking of this period of transition, wrote, "He was seldom seen, never as a performer, in public. His mother alone witnessed to *his perseverance, his indefatigable toil.*"

When he returned to the concert platform he returned a mature artist. "We have heard of Liszt. He can be compared to no other virtuoso. He is the only one of his kind." So wrote Clara Wieck, later Madame Schumann. She continued: "He arouses fright and astonishment, though he is a very lovable artist. His attitude at the piano cannot be described—he is original—he grows somber at the piano. His passion knows no limits. . . . He has a grand spirit. It can be truly said of him that his art is his life."

Liszt's European tours, conducted on a grand scale, brought him homage and acclaim wherever he went. All, from the lowliest peasant to crowned heads in palaces, recognized the supremacy of his artistry. But the memory of these concerts closed with his passing generation. Fortunately for posterity, Liszt composed some excellent music during his sojourns. In these musical travelogues future generations, too, could follow the journeys of this master. One such set was the *Years of Pilgrimage.* On his visits to Italy he wrote others—*Tarantella, Three*

Sonnets by Petrarch, and *Il Penseroso.* The Switzerland group includes *The Bells of Geneva* and *The Chapel of William Tell.*

Liszt was one of the foremost exponents of pictorial or "program music." Even in some of his more pretentious works for orchestra he combines the outline of the symphony with the descriptive element of a story resulting in his symphonic poems. *Les Preludes* is a favorite among music lovers in this style.

From his native Hungary he gathered themes from the folk music of the gypsies—now sad, now wild—and developed them into his exhilarating *Hungarian Rhapsodies.* With the exception of the composer's *Liebestraume,* these rhapsodies are his most familiar music portraits.

In the field of transcriptions he attained an enviable position. Doubtless, many of these works would never have attained renown except for Liszt's meticulous labor of love. He transcribed scores of songs: "Hark! Hark! the Lark," the "Erlking," "Ave Maria," and many others from Schubert's pen; Polish songs, including the "Maiden's Wish" and "My Joys," by Chopin; "Maid of the Ganges," by Mendelssohn; and "Dedication," by Schumann. His paraphrases on the operas of Wagner and Verdi are rather superficial, but even here he did pianists a service, for, in the words of a contemporary pianist, he "got the fingers going." Liszt's command of the piano was such that he discovered and explored every phase of its resources from the subtlest nuances through the most scintillating display of pyrotechnics. Through his playing and in his compositions he established the piano as a miniature orchestra.

Liszt was, beyond question, the most generous musician in all history. He gave benefit concerts whenever the need arose: for the Hungarian flood sufferers when the Danube overflowed; to complete a subscription for the erection of a monument to Beethoven at Bonn; for worthy musicians lacking funds. Whatever the situation, Liszt was ever a true friend in need, stinting neither his time nor his money. When Wagner was exiled and poor, Lizst came to his rescue. He recognized the greatness of the little German composer and ardently championed his cause, even to his own personal detriment. He was willing to take off his own coat of genius that Wagner might walk thereon to greater achievement.

As Liszt grew older, disciples from many lands gathered about him in increasing numbers. The elect of the musical world, Rubinstein, Rosenthal, Tausig, MacDowell, and hundreds of other famous musicians flocked to his Weimar studio to drink in the inspiration of his generous personality, the wealth of his experience, and the authority of his interpretations. One disciple was blind, another had but one arm; but Liszt taught even these to overcome their physical limitations. He went beyond, and aroused the soul of each pupil. One of his American pupils summed up his methods when she wrote, "Under the inspiration of Liszt's playing, everybody worked 'tooth and nail' to achieve the impossible."

On several occasions Edvard Grieg, rising young Norwegian genius, was among the guests. In 1868 the "little Viking," then twenty-five years old, composed his *Concerto in A minor* for piano while spending the summer in a little village in Denmark. Shortly afterward the opportunity came for him to present the manuscript for Liszt's criticism at one of the master's afternoon musicales. In view of the important niche the masterpiece occupies in the repertory of musicians, the occasion has since taken on the nature of the launching of a worthy musical vessel. When all the assembled guests had found their seats, the master, drawing his ecclesiastical robe about him, approached the young Scandinavian visitor, and in his usual cordial manner, asked to see the new score, while the audience sat agape with expectation. Grieg himself describes the episode as follows:

"I had fortunately just received the manuscript of my pianoforte concerto from Leipzig, and took it with me. . . . Winding and I were very anxious to see if he would really play my concerto at sight. I, for my part, considered it impossible; not so Liszt. 'Will you play?' he asked, and I made haste to reply: 'No, I cannot' (you know I never practiced it). Then Liszt took the manuscript, went to the piano, and said to the guests, with his characteristic smile: 'Very well, then, I will show you that I also cannot.' With that he began. I admit that he took the first part of the concerto too fast, and the beginning consequently sounded helter-skelter; but later on, when I had a chance to indicate the tempo, he played as only he can play. It is significant that he played the cadenza, the most difficult part, best of all. His demeanor is worth any price to see. Not content with playing, he at the same time converses and makes comments, addressing a bright remark now to one, now to another of the assembled guests, nodding significantly to the right or left particularly when something pleases him. . . .

"A really divine episode I must not forget. Toward the end of the finale the second theme is, as you may remember, repeated in a mighty fortissimo. In the very last measures, when in the first triplets the first note is changed in the orchestra from G sharp to G, while the piano part, in a mighty scale passage, rushes wildly through the whole reach of the keyboard, he suddenly stopped, rose up to his full height, left the piano, and with big theatric strides and arms uplifted, walked across the large cloister hall, at the same time literally roaring the theme. When he got to the G in question he stretched out his arms imperiously and exclaimed: 'G, G, not G sharp! Splendid!' . . . In conclusion, he handed me the manuscript, and said, in a peculiarly cordial tone: 'Keep steadily on; I tell you, you have the capability, and—do not let them intimidate you.'

"This final admonition was of tremendous importance to me; there was something in it that seemed to give it an air of sanctification. At times, when disappointment and bitterness are in store for me, I shall recall his words, and the remembrance of that hour will have a wonderful power to uphold me in days of adversity."

The master became a legendary figure, the personification of industry, of zeal, of generosity, and of versatility. His vitality was such that at the three-quarter-century mark he appeared at an impromptu gathering in London. H. Klein, an eyewitness,

describes this gathering as follows: "The shout of joy uttered by
the students when he sat down at the piano was something to
remember. It was followed by an intense silence. Then the aged,
but still nimble, fingers ran lightly over the keys, and I was
listening for the first time in my life to Franz Liszt. . . . Even at
seventy-five Liszt was a pianist whose powers lay beyond the
pale to which sober language or calm criticism could reach or
be applied. Enough that his greatest charm seemed to me to lie
in a perfectly divine touch, and in a tone more remarkable for
its exquisitely musical quality than for its volume or dynamic
force, aided by a technique still incomparably brilliant and
superb."

Then suddenly—the end. He was at Bayreuth for the
Wagner festival when he contracted a cold which developed into
double pneumonia. He died the last day of July, 1886.

At forty-five years of age, after a not altogether circumspect
life, he bent his steps toward the Vatican, there to remain for five
years, spending his time in meditation and prayer and in composing along religious lines, and emerged as Abbe Liszt. Many
of his works are religious in style: *Poetic and Religious Harmonies, St. Francis Walking on the Water,* and others.

Liszt had walked in the ways of men. He had known triumph
and failure, riches and poverty, renown and obscurity. He had
lived a full, rich life, but he was not satisfied. Then he sought
to understand the ways of God, and thus found peace and contentment. He learned that music reaches its fullest purpose, not
in self-exaltation but in praise of the Creator and in service to
mankind.

The life of Liszt was a wellspring of abundance. He was
bountifully endowed; he bountifully gave. The generous measure of his gifts was lavishly meted out to others from the mu-
nificence of his great heart. At the very height of his musical
triumphs he relinquished, with characteristic altruism, his un-
challenged right to the crown among concert pianists to devote
himself to creative work and teaching. Thereafter, for nearly half
his lifetime, he spent a considerable share of his time and energy

in imparting to others the secrets of his impeccable virtuosity and of his unique approach to the hidden beauties in the works of the old masters. In selfless devotion to the art he made plain the scope, the purpose, and the verities of music to those who were fortunate to come under his tutelage; and then they in turn went abroad to spread the new light.

Although Franz Liszt won a place as a favored master among the nobility of music, he willingly assumed the role of a music servant that he might thereby enlarge his usefulness in declaring music's mission to the world. This was true greatness. "The greatest thing a human soul ever does in this world is to see something and tell what he sees in a plain way." (Ruskin.) The most far-reaching effect of Liszt's service resulted from his part in establishing music as a cosmopolitan art, the natural heritage of all men. One music lover expressed the feelings of many who have caught the light when he wrote, "The greatest and best in music is ours if we will but try to understand it, and once attained, no power can take it from us."

Johannes Brahms

Johannes Brahms

1833-1897

He Chiseled in Granite

∽

HE CAME from the slums. His baby days were spent in a tenement in the poorest district of old Hamburg. His father, Jakob Brahms, had settled in this port city on the Elbe after roving the country as an amateur musician. Here he played the contrabass in the municipal theater. He was generally good natured, but he was decidedly independent. During a rehearsal, when the orchestral conductor singled him out as playing too loud, he vehemently countered, *"Herr Kapellmeister,* this is my contrabass, and I shall play on it as loud as I please."

The house where Jakob Brahms boarded was kept by a little, plain, ailing woman. Whether it was through her motherly ways or her exceptional ability to cook delicious meals, she cast a magic spell over the twenty-four-year-old lad. After just a week's residence he led his forty-one-year-old landlady to the altar.

Johannes was the second of three children. For all their meager fare and damp, poorly furnished living rooms, the early days of the family were happy ones. Johannes loved to marshal his colored lead soldiers into military positions, in anticipation, as it were, of days to come, when he would marshal the hosts of sound with rhythmic precision.

A delightful surprise awaited Papa Brahms one day as he was giving Johannes his piano lesson. While naming the keys the five-year-old boy suddenly turned to look out the window, in the meantime continuing to name the keys. This led his father to test him further, and thus he found that Johannes was gifted with absolute pitch. But this was only the beginning of his gifts.

The news of Johannes's swift musical progress was spread abroad, and offers came to the family for him to make a concert tour extending as far as America. Fortunately his broad-minded parents did not succumb to the lure of exploitation, but declined the offer, much as they needed what financial gain the tour would have brought. Instead, Johannes continued his training with teachers at Hamburg.

The Brahmses clutched the frazzled end of Fortune's rope. The soup was thin. The rooms were often uncomfortably cold in winter. It became necessary for the children to find odd jobs to help support the family. Johannes, only nine, began playing in dance halls and taverns of the harbor, often into the small hours of the morning. He was thus exposed to life's sordid side in his most impressionable years; further, he heard the poorest type of music as he pounded out the dance tunes for the scuffling feet of drunken sailors and their partners. This irregular program taxed his delicate health, and he became anemic and suffered from severe headaches.

As a lad of fourteen Johannes was invited to visit a friend living in a little town about sixty miles from Hamburg. This jaunt into the country proved a most fortunate change. He caught his first glimpse of a new world and of better things as he passed through the fields and forests. His health, too, was restored during his sojourn at Winsen.

In his later teens Johannes threw himself into whatever tasks he could find to make his living. He was an early riser. "The best songs come into my mind," he said, "while brushing my shoes before daybreak." He gave lessons, continued to play at dance halls, and wrote hack music under a pen name. Then he chanced to meet the Hungarian violinist Remenyi, and played some accompaniments for him. The two became friendly and decided to travel together from town to town. At least the concerts they planned to give would earn their expenses. So, vagabondlike, they ventured forth, prepared for any emergency. When, at one city, the piano was tuned a half tone too low, Brahms, with his customary ease, transposed the *Kreutzer Sonata* of Beethoven a half tone higher. The eminent violinist Joachim was in the audience and was immediately impressed by the pianistic skill of the accompanist. Later Johannes played his *Scherzo, Opus 4* for Joachim. As a result a friendship developed between the musicians that lasted a lifetime. Joachim was one of the first links in the chain of Brahms's associates who set his fire of genius aglow.

Then Remenyi broke relations with Brahms, saying curtly, "I have no more desire to wander as a musical beggar from village to village. You may try your luck alone." But Brahms was not dependent upon sheer luck to carry him through. He had come from rugged peasant stock with a will to work; his genius and training were sound; and he was acquiring new and finer friendships that would inspire him to his best achievements.

With Joachim's letter of introduction in his portfolio, Brahms set out to visit Liszt at Weimar. The wizard of the piano welcomed him in his usual cordial manner, and the two played for each other. Each was a genius in his way, although they were opposites in nature and style. Liszt enjoyed soaring into the musical stratosphere, while Brahms preferred descending into the musical deep. Brahms would never become one of the many ardent disciples surrounding the Weimar master. Though they parted with a vigorous handclasp they were still strangers.

Young Brahms found the friendship of the Schumanns much more to his liking. He made it a point while passing through Dusseldorf, where they then lived, to pay them a visit. Robert Schumann, then in his early forties, welcomed the youth of twenty with open arms. Shortly after he began to play one of his own sonatas at the request of Schumann, his host broke into the performance and exclaimed, "Clara must hear this!" When his pianist-wife entered the room, Schumann further exclaimed, "Now you shall hear such music, my dear Clara, as you have never heard! Young man, begin the piece again!"

And so one of the great friendships of music was born. Schumann's enthusiasm for the newcomer culminated in an article, written in his journal, announcing the advent of this "new prophet John." Under the title "New Paths," Schumann, among other things, wrote: "It seemed to me . . . that a musician would inevitably appear to whom it was vouchsafed to give the highest and most ideal expression to the tendencies of the time, one who would not show us his mastery in a gradual development, but, like Minerva, would spring fully armed from the head of Jove. And he has come, a young man over whose cradle graces and heroes kept watch. His name is Johannes Brahms, and he comes from Hamburg."

The wholesome spirit of brotherhood in art as reflected in Schumann's heraldry of the then-unknown Brahms, is a lesson on true greatness. All men may not have an equal measure of gifts such as Schumann had, but whoever wishes may emulate his altruistic spirit. Many noble lives, many great deeds, many masterpieces, owe their inspiration to the kindness and the encouragement of a friend.

Brahms profited immeasurably by the endorsement of his older contemporary. Publishers accepted his manuscripts unhesitatingly. The public eagerly awaited his works. Then a new controversy regarding the relative merits of his most recent compositions would inevitably follow. Several appointments came his way, including that of director of the court concerts of the prince of Detmold, which Brahms accepted. The composer stayed here four years and then returned to Hamburg. He made occasional public appearances as conductor or as pianist. In the role of pianist he was forceful rather than accurate. It is very often the case that the composer is not his own best interpreter. However, Brahms introduced many of his new works on these rare appearances.

When, at twenty-nine, Brahms moved to Vienna, he adopted the Austrian capital as his home for the remainder of his days and adopted, likewise, many of the characteristics of Hungarian music. These styles flavor a number of his works such as the *G minor Quartet*, the two serenades for orchestra, *Opera 11* and *Opera 16*, besides his stirring Hungarian dances.

For thirty-five years Mother Vienna was to look upon this homespun, interesting, often eccentric foster son. She would learn to know his inner self, his modesty, his love of children, his wit, his depth of thought. She would testify that he remained a student throughout his life, that he was one of the most logical and self-critical of all the masters. She observed that behind his austere appearance there beat a tender, human heart. Though his hands were "rough and hard as files" there welled in the ruth of his eyes the "Cradle Song" so tenderly lyric as to stand alone in its class.

Brahms became a celebrity in Vienna and in the whole music world, but he never lost sight of his humble origin. He loved his parents and often sent them gifts, although toward himself he dealt most niggardly. His *German Requiem* was written in memory of the passing of his mother.

He remained a bachelor throughout his life. He had several love affairs and wrote beautiful love songs, but he always stopped short of marriage.

One of Brahms' biographers gave a straightforward glimpse of the character of the composer, as both man and artist, when he wrote: "It is impossible to imagine Brahms manicured and scented, and though he was of the most scrupulous cleanliness in body and dress, he always had the appearance of one who washes with common soap at the pump, and knew nothing of pomatums and perfumes."

The composer cut a rather droll figure as he sauntered down the street in his "high-water" trousers, over his shoulders a plaid shawl fastened in front with a large safety pin, and a derby hat. His short, paunchy build contributed to his wheezing in loco-motion. That patriarchal beard, grown at forty-five, was, more than likely, a shrubbery of camouflage, inasmuch as he detested wearing neckties. His rooms, too, were typical bachelor quarters. Music and books were littered everywhere. In one corner stood his innocent-looking trick rocker. As the unsuspecting guest sat down either he would tumble onto the floor or his feet would fly into the air. If Brahms had to make a trip, he would throw his wardrobe helter-skelter into the trunk. But out of the chaos of his living quarters he brought out orderly, logical, beautiful music.

The master was fond of food—and drinks. One restaurant, the Red Hedgehog, was a particular favorite with him. Beethoven and Schubert had eaten here. The place seemed to glow with reminiscences of the great in music. Here Brahms exchanged wit with Dvorak, the composer of the *New World Symphony* and the little "Humoresque"; with Johann Strauss, the waltz king; with Von Bulow, the pianist-conductor; and others. Here he found respite from the intense concentration necessary to the production of a masterpiece.

After Brahms had settled in Vienna he seldom went elsewhere except for occasional concert tours to Holland, Switzerland, and Germany, and short holiday excursions. The children about the street came to know and love him. They understood that under the shaggy bearlike exterior was the heart of a lamb. They knew that the bulging pockets of his shabby coat were likely to hold candy or some coins for them. And invariably the poorest children were the object of his kindnesses. Biographer Robert Schauffler gives a word picture of Brahms as the children's friend in the lines following:

YULE FIRE IN A SLUM

"Between a refuse pile and a pedlar's tray,
I saw pale children circling, hand in hand,
Round a green branch—their gutter fairyland.
Deep in the slush they frolicked, lost in play,
For this was all the Christmas tree they had:
A scrap of wilted pine. They had made it glad

With paper ribbons full of glorious holes—
The spoil of broken piano-player rolls:
Festoons of silent music, draped among
The twigs where toys and candy should have hung.
'Let's make it burn!' The tiny blaze leaped higher.
Their Christmas tree was now their Christmas fire.
And, in the sudden glare, I could plainly see,
Printed upon a burning paper's end:
'Johannes Brahms . . . *G minor Rhapsody.*'

"I thought how it would please that children's friend
If he could watch his flaming tones achieve
Such radiance for a gutter Chrismas Eve;
Though rhapsodies must, phoenixlike, progress
Into another form of loveliness.
How that Pied Piper's coattails would grow fat
With sugar toys; how every bright-eyed brat
Would encore 'Uncle Bahms' with crow and shout!

. . . . .

Children, is there a candy shop about?"

But it is not given to children to grasp the meaning of his
music. That, with the exception of a few short pieces, must be
left for mature minds. His music, ranging from the simple folkmusic style through the most erudite symphonies, is often on
first hearing ·considered dry and academic. But when it is re
heard its dynamic depth and inner beauty come to light.

Brahms is classed with Bach and Beethoven as one of the
three B's in music. He combines salient qualities of both these
masters with the deeper expression of romanticism. He, as was
the case with Bach and Beethoven, was not tempted by mere
sensuous beauty, nor did he strive for effect. His music is never
superficial, but thorough and intellectual, and built to endure.

In his music—including the intermezzi, the capriccios, the
rhapsodies, the sonatas, and up through the symphonies—new
and complex rhythms, new harmonic textures, new technical
difficulties, are earmarks of his original style. Consistently he
draws the waters of his inspiration from solid rock. Only occasionally does he relax and appear in a playful mood as in his

Waltzes Opus 39 and in the *Hungarian Dances.* Four great
symphonies, the *Tragic Overture* and the *Academic Festival
Overture,* fine choral works, and about two hundred songs add
to his glory as a sculptor in tone.

Throughout his middle and later life Brahms enjoyed robust
health, but toward his sixty-fourth year a liver ailment began to
give him distress. A consultation with his physician revealed a
malignant condition. His rotund figure soon wasted, his color
changed, and he became bedridden. When, on his deathbed, a
friend brought him a drink to slake his thirst, the dying master
gratefully whispered, "Yes, that is beautiful." These were his
last words. In contrast with the penury of the earlier masters,
Brahms left, aside from the inestimable legacy of his masterpieces,
about one hundred thousand dollars to his heirs.

The art of Brahms is noteworthy for the nice balance maintained therein between musical thought and musical feeling.
He was one of the most scholarly of the masters and also one
of the most profound in his expression of human emotion and experience. He had been thoroughly schooled in the best classical
traditions of Bach and Beethoven, and he adopted their models
of symmetrical design as a vehicle for expressing the individuality
and integrity of his own personality. His music endures by reason
of its perfection of form, its nobility of thought, and its sincere
expression of musical truth.

Brahms was another link in the chain of geniuses that have
made musical art the accumulated wealth of centuries in intellectual and emotional idealism. Men of genius, as a group,
are a singular manifestation of God's creative power. They are
"instruments used by God wherewith to improve mankind."
They live in a world apart. They breathe the rarefied air of the
mountaintop. Theirs is the task of bringing advance light to
the world. Theirs are the privations and pains, the sorrows and the
joys, the solitude and absorbing passion that attend the creative
process in great works of art. Their gifts enable them adequately
to express that universal search for truth and beauty, for love
of freedom, for brotherhood.

Peter Ilich Tchaikovsky

1840-1893

And if I laugh at any mortal thing,
'Tis that I may not weep.—LORD BYRON.

*ETER, seven and winsome, was patriotic to the marrow
of his bones. It was in the midst of a geography lesson that he,
moved by an irresistible impulse and unable to keep his feelings
to himself, suddenly showered the map of Russia with kisses,
and then spat on the other countries. When his teacher, who was
French, remonstrated, he managed to mix a little diplomacy
with his ire, as he replied, "Don't you see I have covered France
with my hand!"

Peter's home, near the foothills of the Ural Mountains, was
large and comfortable, and boasted such luxuries as a comple-
ment of servants, tutors, and a governess. His father managed a
government copper mine and, consequently, enjoyed a high
standing in the district. Peter had a lovable nature, although he
was careless in his habits, and from the time he was five years
old he was eager to learn. Neither his father nor his mother was
musical, and therefore, when their little Ilich began craving
an outlet for his musical feelings, they could not quite understand it. The other six children did not crave one; why should
he? The parents decided to discourage his inclinations. They

purposed further that when he grew older he should study law.

They consented, however, when he reached the age of eight years, to give him music lessons, not realizing to what ends this would eventually lead. His teachers seemed not to detect any particular talent in Peter; one, in reply to his father's query, even advised against a musical career for him. While he wrote some dance music and improvised, his musical progress was not extraordinary.

Peter's mother died from cholera when he was but fourteen years old. This deeply wounded his already shy, melancholy, and sensitive nature. But he was able to stifle his feelings and pursue his legal studies, already begun at the school of jurisprudence in Petrograd (present Leningrad). By the time he was nineteen he had graduated and received an appointment in the ministry of justice. But his heart was not in his work. He had heard a strange call, and he yearned to answer.

Then the giant within him awoke. The cords that had bound him were beginning to slacken, and the day was approaching when he would lead a phalanx of majors and minors into the sunshine of a new day. In his early twenties he entered the conservatory at Petrograd (Leningrad), a "free" man at last.

He knew, however, that even at his age, he was still just a "fledgling"; he had yet to try his wings. "Do not think for a moment," he wrote his sister, "that I expect ever to be a great artist. I merely had to do what I felt was my calling. Whether I become a famous composer or a poor music teacher is indifferent to me, at all events my conscience will be clear, and I shall no longer have the right to complain about my lot."

Peter's resolve "to be a good musician and earn my daily bread" was soon put to a test in his student days. Long hours of study while subsisting on a very small income tried his endurance as well as his economy. So when he graduated at twenty-five, his cantata on Schiller's *Ode to Joy* doubtless reflected his own feeling of joy and satisfaction.

Nicholas Rubinstein, brother of the noted pianist Anton Rubinstein, was at the time the director of the Moscow Conservatorium. Though he was overbearing and quick tempered, his loyalty to Tchaikovsky grew through the years and singularly influenced the composer's life. Rubinstein invited him to teach harmony in his conservatory and to live in his own home. Moreover, he brought out many of Tchaikovsky's compositions, and because of his own influential position, was able to procure a "fairy godmother" for the young, inexperienced teacher.

Rubinstein had made the acquaintance of a Mme. von Meck, a widow living in Moscow, not far from the conservatory. She was the mother of eleven children; she was shrewd, shy, and fabulously wealthy. Mme. von Meck held herself aloof from society, and few there were, outside of her immediate family, who passed the portals into her sumptuous mansion. Nicholas Rubinstein was one of the few. His visits generally revolved around their common interest—music.

On a winter day in 1876 Rubinstein stuffed the orchestral fantasia *The Tempest* into his brief case and headed for the mansion. Formalities ended, he made known his mission. He had come to gain assistance for a poor, worthy youth of musical promise. As Rubinstein was an excellent pianist, he played selections from *The Tempest* and then eloquently pleaded the cause of Peter Ilich. But it was the music that won her heart. Then and there she promised to commission the composer.

Thus began one of the strangest romances, if romance it was, in the annals of music. Mme. von Meck opened the volume of correspondence that was to take place between them, by commissioning him to write a new composition and stipulating, among other things, that they should never meet. For more than a dozen years they poured their innermost feelings into these letters; the letters became a release for two shy natures, two bleeding hearts.

In consequence of Mme. von Meck's generosity the composer was free to devote his entire energies to creative work, unhampered by financial worries or petty duties. Music poured from his pen. Songs, quartets, overtures—including the *Romeo and*

Juliet and the *1812* overture—and symphonies, through the *Fifth*, were written before the composer was forty years old. The *Fourth Symphony*, dedicated to Mme. von Meck, bears the inscription "My Best Friend." In regard to the program of the fourth movement, he wrote her further, "If you truly find no joy within yourself, look for it in others." Then, after commenting on the joyous peasant festival depicted in the music, he concluded, "And how fortunate to be ruled by such simple immediate feelings. Here one sees the existence of simple, deep joys; enter into them and life will be bearable." Mme. von Meck was overjoyed on hearing the symphony, and happy that it was dedicated to her.

In contrast with Mme. von Meck's grateful reception of this dedication was that afforded the *Piano Concerto in B-flat minor* by Nicholas Rubinstein, to whom it was first dedicated. His derogatory attitude is the more interesting, in view of the mounting acceptance of the work since that time. Tchaikovsky related how he first brought the work to Rubinstein and how the latter listened without comment to the entire concerto. "Then," in the words of the composer, "sprang forth a vigorous stream of words from Rubinstein's mouth. At first he spoke quietly, but by degrees his passion rose, and finally he resembled Zeus hurling thunderbolts. It appeared that my concerto was worthless and absolutely unplayable, that the passages were manufactured and withal so clumsy as to be beyond correction, that the composition itself was bad, trivial, and commonplace, that I had stolen this point from somebody, and that from somebody else, and that only two or three pages had any value, and all the rest should be either destroyed or entirely remodeled. . . . In short, an unbiased spectator of the scene could only have thought that I was a stupid, untalented, and conceited spoiler of music paper, who had had the impertinence to show his rubbish to a celebrated man." Instead of changing the music the composer changed the dedication, Bulow, contemporary pianist, being the appreciative recipient. Rubinstein later repented his harsh criticism and apologized to the master.

In spite of Tchaikovsky's shyness and melancholy, he was a lovable, tender soul and not without a sense of humor. These qualities are reflected in much of his music. Sometimes both sides of his nature seem alternately to vie with each other for supremacy. His ballets, notably the vivacious *Nutcracker Suite*, picture his happy side. This suite, based on a fairy story, relates the adventures of a little girl who had received a nutcracker as a Christmas gift. In a dream she sees her nutcracker metamorphosed into a prince, who escorts her on a visit to jam mountain. She is there welcomed by the sugar-plum fairy, who entertains her with dances by various Christmas toys, beginning with the sugar-plum fairy's own dance and closing with the "Waltz of the Flowers." The picturesque orchestration gives the music a captivating charm.

At thirty-seven Peter Ilich decided he should marry, or rather, his fiancee made the decision for him. For some time she had written him ardent love letters, and although it is very evident that Tchaikovsky was never in love with her, he seemed to lack the courage to break relations with her, and soon found himself engaged. They were married and lived unhappily together for less than ten days. Then they separated.

The experience was like a bad dream from which the composer would be long in recovering. He sought an escape in travel. He wrote long letters to Mme. von Meck and unburdened his feelings. But his most effective escape was found in work. "So I turn like a squirrel in a wheel," he wrote, "I work as hard as I can. . . . My work alone saves me. And I work."

A genius at work becomes a veritable powerhouse of concentrated energy. What takes place in his mind as he works? Tchaikovsky, in the following intimate paragraphs, reveals the answer, at least as far as he was concerned.

"Generally the germ of the work appears with lightning suddenness, quite unexpectedly. If this germ falls on fertile soil— that is to say, when the desire to work is felt—it takes root with incredible strength and rapidity, shoots up from twigs, leaves, and finally blossoms. I cannot describe the process of creation otherwise than by this comparison. The greatest difficulty lies in the necessity that the germ should appear under favorable circumstances; then everything will proceed of its own accord.

"It would be vain in me to endeavor to express in words that immeasurable sense of happiness which comes over me when a new thought appears and begins to grow into definite forms. I then forget everything and behave as if I were mad; all in me pulsates and vibrates; scarcely have I begun the sketches when thousands of details are chasing each other through my brain.

"In the midst of this magic process it sometimes happens that some shock from without tears me from my somnambulism—as for instance if someone suddenly rings, or if a servant enters the room, or if the clock strikes and reminds me that it is time to stop. . . . Such disturbances are absolutely terrible! Sometimes they frighten inspiration away for a time, and I must seek for it again, often in vain. In that case cold reason and technical resources have to be called in to assist."

Tchaikovsky put his very life into his music—his dreams, his tears, his soul. He did not write to become famous, but fame was inevitable. His compositions were sought by leading publishers. Performances of his works drew capacity audiences. He toured Europe and America in a succession of triumphs. But when fame reached its height, a new disappointment came that almost crushed him. As strangely as they had begun, the letters from his patroness, Mme. von Meck, suddenly ceased. The friend of his triumphs and disappointments, for some unknown reason, had severed connections with him. So, with all the world bowing at his feet, he was still—alone.

Again his spirit was revived by diligent work. A new symphony, his sixth, began to take shape. The composer drew from his accumulated creative resources and varied life-experiences and molded them into this symphony. When completed he called it the *Symphonie Pathetique*. It was a review, so to speak, of the closing chapters of his pathetic life. Herein trickled his bitter tears; herein flowed the pathos of his broken heart.

Would there be a seventh symphony? What would be the trend of his next creation. Were his creative powers declining? What did the future hold? The answer lay in the contents of a lifted glass. It appeared to contain a draft of refreshing water but contained instead a fatal potion. The cholera season was at its height, and it was necessary that all drinking water be boiled. In a moment of relaxed vigilance the composer had failed to take this precaution, and pressed the cup to his lips. As he was not in good health at the time, the contaminated water soon took its toll. The dread disease, of which his mother had died brought him to his death at the age of fifty-three.

Tchaikovsky attained an honored place among the great masters of music. His works form the closing chapters of romanticism. In later composers music would follow new trends, away from the classical and purely emotional styles into modernism in its various ramifications. Music marches on. Masterpieces are still being written, in spite of rampant fear and hate and war. The exigence of the times serves but to increase the creative urge among those having a proclivity for musical expression. During the first world war Sibelius wrote his *Fifth Symphony,* "in which the master's creative spirit soared like an eagle in the sun above a tortured and broken world." During the second world war Shostakovich wrote his *Seventh Symphony* in the midst of fire and shell, while engaged as a fire warden during the siege of Leningrad.

The tendencies of the present day are discernible in the musical utterances of modern composers. A world that is constantly changing its concepts of spiritual values and material accomplishments faithfully reflects itself in similar cycles of changes in its music. These changes in art, interesting and worthy as they are, only bring into bolder relief the greatness of the older masters. The works of the dozen high-ranking composers from Bach to Tchaikovsky form the grandest mountain range in musical history. Their consummate achievements, begun in the valleys of the needs and difficulties of humankind, rose triumphantly to the courage and joy of its mountaintops.

9

He who would scale their heights and reach their summits, has set for himself a formidable goal.

For the purpose of recapitulation let us forget for a few moments that more than two centuries are spanned from the birth of Bach in 1685 to the death of Tchaikovsky in 1893, and imagine that they are living contemporaries who will appear before us in an impromptu gathering to conduct a panel discussion on music.

The curtains are drawn aside; the twelve apostles of the gospel of music take their places around a table. Bach—Christian, solid citizen, fountainhead of music—is the special guest of honor. He is greeting Handel for the first time, although they were born within a few days of each other and but a few miles apart. Mendelssohn, one of Bach's most faithful disciples, is especially solicitous of the welfare of the Eisenach master. Beethoven—dour-visaged, stoical—flanks Bach on his right.

The assembly presents an interesting study in contrasting personalities, from the gaunt figure of Chopin to the portliness of Handel; from the careless attire of Brahms to the sartorial resplendence of Mozart; from the ruefulness of Tchaikovsky to the effervescent cheerfulness of Haydn; from the reticence of the poet-composer Schumann to the amiable sociability of Mendelssohn.

Schumann's toast to Bach, which he concludes by declaring with emphasis that he is "neither ancient nor modern, but much more—eternal" is followed by several warmhearted eulogies to the Weimar cantor. Though they do not see eye to eye on many points, they are in almost unanimous agreement that Bach is the greatest of them all.

Inasmuch as all present are fine keyboard instrumentalists, most of them pianists, the man who is recognized as the greatest pianist of all time is requested to tell what the piano has meant to him. Master of wit alike in speech or in the language of tone, Liszt unhesitatingly responds:

"My piano is to me as his boat to a seaman. It is as his horse to the Arab. Nay, it has been my vision, my speech, my breath of life. Its strings have thrilled with my passions; its keys have obeyed my every caprice. Perhaps the tie which secretly binds us so closely together is a delusion, but my piano is the child of my heart."

The phase of music that is being stressed particularly, concerns its purposes and objectives as related to the needs of a complex society. Beethoven has laid aside his usual demure manner and now rises to comment: "Music is the mediator between the spiritual and the sensual life." Bach immediately follows with the observation so characteristic of him: "The object of all music should be the glory of God." And now is heard the lisping voice of Mendelssohn, saying with deep conviction, "What a divine calling is music! Though everything else may appear shallow and repulsive, even the smallest task in music is so absorbing and carries us so far away from town, country and earth and all worldly things, that it is truly a blessed gift of God."

It is significant that the masters, living close to the heart of music, regarded it as a tie that, next to religion, binds the human with the divine. Their burden was to keep the art unsullied; to retain for posterity only works of sterling worth; and it was of greatest concern to them that music should be cherished not only by the musically elect but also by men, women, and children in all walks of life. They regarded music, "not as a convenient method of securing selfish advantage and sterile fame, but as a sympathetic bond of union between human beings."

The gathering disperses. The curtains lower. As they depart—the poets, the prophets, the philosophers, and the philanthropists of music—they leave a benediction of fine music that fills the room with a flood of glorious light.

Brethren all, they had partaken of all the weaknesses and trials and pains common to the human family. Masters all, they brought beauty out of the ashes of poverty, suffering, and misfortune.

Edvard Grieg

1843-1907

Dark and true and tender is the North.—TENNYSON.

NORWAY—land of crystal-clear fiords and verdure-clad, snow-capped mountains, of midnight sun and northern lights; land of legendary sagas, of trolls and gnomes; land of simple fisherfolk and industrious peasants; land of traditional religion and intersocial integrity—this was the land of Grieg's nativity, this was the land that fulfilled his heart's desires.

Between Grieg and Norway there existed a filial bond as tender as that between a mother and her only son. Grieg was nurtured at her bosom. In his childhood he learned to know and love the robust strength and rustic beauty of her rugged terrain. He sojourned in Germany, Denmark, and Italy eight years for study and self-development; but it was on his return to his native land that he found himself—found the role he was to play in "kindling the northern lights" until all the world would behold the effulgence of its glow. His music became saturated with the fresh vigor of the North Sea; it diffused the tangy fragrance of Norway's pine woods. He spent his golden, ripening years close to the heart of his mother country, and on his death was buried in the cleft of a rock overlooking one of her numerous fiords.

The seaport city of Bergen, where Grieg was born, reaches back a thousand years into the past, when it was founded by King Olav Kyrre, as he plied the waters along the coastline in his Viking ship. Access to the city, other than by boat, is difficult. Landward, the city is surrounded by seven mountains, tireless sentinels jealously guarding the many red-roofed dwellings sprawled over the city and crawling up onto the mountainsides.

Visitors approaching the harbor are overawed by a view that is unique as picturesque cities go. The scene so touched Bjornstjerne Bjornson on his first visit that he was moved to write stirring patriotic sentiments which crystallized into the national anthem: *Ja, vi elsker detta landet!*

From the encircling mountains pointing, as it were, into the legendary past, down to the busy harbor with its fish market and shipping docks, and out over the beckoning, unknown waters, Bergen, as a setting for Edvard Grieg's early home life, came to mean more than the city of his childhood—it became to him a perpetual fount of inspiration. Many years later, on the occasion of the composer's sixtieth birthday, he stressed this point when he said, "Bergen's environment—the life of its people, Bergen's exploits and enterprizes of every kind have inspired me."

More immediately influencing the course of his life was the musical atmosphere of his home. To his mother, Edvard owed his proclivity for music and his love of nature. Strandgaten, No. 152, where the Griegs lived with their five children, was thrown open once each week to their friends who loved music, and Mme. Grieg would take part, not only in acting the gracious hostess, but in playing and singing from the works of Mozart, Weber, and others of the classic and romantic composers.

When he was five little Edvard began to make some musical discoveries of his own. He later wrote of "the wonderful, mysterious satisfaction with which my arms stretched out to the piano to discover—not a melody; that was far off—no; that there is such a thing as harmony. First a third, then a chord of three notes, then a full chord of four, ending at last with both hands. Oh, joy! a combination of five, the chord of the ninth. When I found that out, my happiness knew no bounds." At six his music lessons with his mother began. Edvard would rather dream than ply his little given tasks, and so an important phase of Mme. Grieg's teaching was that of setting his sails. Now and again she would relate stories about another Norwegian lad, also a native of Bergen, who by faithful practice had become world-famous through his beautiful violin playing. The stories so charmed Edvard that in imagination he came to look upon Ole Bull not only as an idol but as a god. In him he found a new inspiration.

On a beautiful summer day, when Edvard was fifteen and the Griegs were living on their country estate near Bergen, Edvard observed a rider bring his galloping horse to a halt and dismount in front of the house. A thrill like an electric current took hold of Edvard. It was the "idol of his dreams"—Ole Bull.

Ole Bull was a romantic figure in any company, a typical Norseman—tall, athletic, flaxen-haired, blue-eyed, courageous, independent, and headstrong. He was a Peer Gynt of the flesh. He it was of whom Longfellow wrote in his "Tales of a Wayside Inn."

His career, beginning as a minstrel wandering from town to town in Norway, culminated in a sphere of influence that covered the Old and New World, where he filled concert halls everywhere and won acclaim as a natural poetic genius of the violin— all the more remarkable in that he was almost entirely self-taught.

Edvard's contact with Bull was most fortunate at this time. Bull, older than Grieg by thirty-three years, inspired the youth with tales of his musical exploits, with his laurels fresh from recent musical conquests, and more especially, by the virtuoso's enthusiasm for his Norse homeland, her natural countryside, her folklore and folkmusic, and her people. "Do you see the fjelder there?" he would say. "The lakes and streams, the valleys and the forests and the blue sky over all, have made my music, not I. So it is frequently when I am playing, it seems as if I merely made mechanical motions and were only a silent listener while the Soul of Norway sings in my soul." Bull's style is available to posterity in his only melodic creation now extant, *Saetergirl's Sunday*. It is singularly charming in its plaintive tenderness, depicting the lonely vigil of a Norwegian shepherd girl as she longs for home and loved ones.

Bull in turn grew enthusiastic on hearing what Edvard had already done in composition, and suggested to his parents that they allow the boy to follow music's calling and go on to Germany for study.

Bull's impress on the design of Edvard's life was to be deep and lasting. His suggestion that Edvard proceed at once to Leipzig to study at the conservatory was summarily followed; arrangements were soon made, and the lad, feeling "like a parcel stuffed with dreams," was on the North Sea bound for the music center of Germany. His feelings, on arrival in the city, were a strange mixture of awe, occasioned by the strange atmosphere of the city, of joyful anticipation, and of homesickness.

The Leipzig Conservatorium was founded by Mendelssohn in 1843. Its brilliant teaching staff then included Robert Schumann, who taught score-reading there for a short period. The school boasted musicians such as Moscheles and Reinecke at the time Edvard became a student there. With some of his teachers Edvard was well pleased; with others he decried their pedantry; and with still others he felt like a spirited race horse that was being checked too closely by the reins. One teacher, however, stood out above the others in the measure of friendly encouragement he gave Edvard. Grieg's own account of his first meeting with this teacher is interesting in that it shows how highly human friendship and encouragement are valued even in the life of a genius. He wrote:

"Before I knew Hauptmann—I was not yet sixteen and still wore my child's blouse—I had attained in *Privatprufung* [a kind of yearly private examination in which all the pupils, without exception, had to take part] the honor of being allowed to play a piano piece of my own composition. When I had finished and left the piano, I saw to my great surprise an elderly gentleman get up from the teacher's table and come towards me. He laid his hand on my shoulder and said only, 'Good day, my boy. We must be good friends.' It was Hauptmann. Naturally I loved him from that moment. Ill as he was in the last year of his life, he gave lessons at his home, the Thomasschule, Sebastian Bach's old residence. Here I had the happiness of getting to know him more intimately. I remember him on his sofa in dressing gown and slippers, his spectacles almost touching my book of studies, which still retains more than one spot of the yellow brown snuff that was always dripping from his snuffy nose. He used to sit with a big silk handkerchief in his hand so as to forestall the drops. But he had no luck. Then it was used as a cloth to wipe the book of studies, where its traces are still plain to see."

English students at the school included Arthur Sullivan, whose small works "The Lost Chord" and "Onward Christian Soldiers" are universally known. During a performance of Mendelssohn's *St. Paul* it was Edvard's pleasure to sit next to Sullivan and follow the score. Together they reverently turned the pages from Mendelssohn's own manuscript. From these fellow students Edvard learned what he had failed to realize heretofore: the necessity of submission to the routine of study. He thereupon unwisely went to the other extreme of injudiciously applying himself to his studies until he suffered a physical collapse. This illness so impaired his health that for the balance of his life he had but one lung. On learning of his illness, his mother hastened to his side, and after consultation, found it wise to take her son back to Bergen, where he gradually improved.

The youth returned to Leipzig after a short time, although his parents wished him to stay on in Bergen throughout the following winter to recuperate fully. For several years he threw his depleted energies into his work, and graduated with credit at the age of nineteen.

His stay at Leipzig gave him a thorough acquaintance with the classical structure, as was later evidenced in his adoption of the sonata form in works such as his *Piano Sonata in E minor,* his sonatas for piano and violin, and his *Piano Concerto in A minor* and even in the antique style of the *Holberg Suite.* He acquired, too, the romantic spirit as expressed in the works of Mendelssohn, Schumann, and Chopin. "The melodic richness of these masters, their luxuriant harmonies and short mosaic-like forms satisfied the needs of Grieg's disposition to the full."

And then—northward! He spent the summer vacationing in Norway, after which he took up residence in Copenhagen, Denmark, for further study. Here he came under the influence of Gade, the founder of the Scandinavian school, and Hans Christian Andersen, Danish poet and author of many fairy tales. The youthful Grieg set fifteen of Andersen's poems to music.

As Edvard's love of music led him onward in his pursuit of his lifework, Denmark came to assume a particular importance to him, for it was here that the youth first heard the music of love. Edvard met Nina Hagerup while visiting relatives in the Kronborg Castle farm near Helsingor. He was twenty; she was eighteen. The Hagerups, also of Bergen, had moved about ten years earlier to Denmark. Nina was a talented little maid with a lovely voice and a flair for dramatic expression. They were engaged the following year, and in this same year Edvard composed his most famous song, *"Ich liebe dich."* However, as is often the case with poor composers, there was opposition to their marriage, especially on the part of Nina's mother, who said of the prospective groom, "He is nobody, he has nothing, and he writes music that nobody cares to listen to." They waited three years before love triumphed over outside hindrances.

Grieg's parents had followed with keen interest the successes of their son, and were happy to make any necessary sacrifice to support him in his student days in Germany, Denmark, and later in Rome. Mme. Grieg at this time even gave up her grand piano in helping the newly married couple to furnish their home. And as those were days when practical handmade gifts, especially knitted socks, were in vogue, she saw to it that the

groom received his just share. In a letter accompanying the gifts
Mme. Grieg wrote, "The grey stockings are the sixth pair I have
found time to knit this autumn to fit you out at starting. The
striped ones I thought might be the wedding socks, if you have
nothing better. . . . My prayers and good wishes are knitted
into them."

The sense of gratification that the Griegs continued to
show in the progress and success of their son must have been
a silent inspiration to him throughout his lifetime. When Grieg
sent his parents a telegram telling them that his first concert in
Oslo was a success, he soon after received a letter from his
youngest sister, Elizabeth, replying: "I have never seen father
and mother so happy; father rushed like a boy with the telegram
first into the kitchen to mother, then up to John, then to the
back drawing-room, and finally to the attic, to tell everyone in
the house himself. It was a happy day—happier than our house
had known for a very long time."

It was not in a spirit of arrogance that they enjoyed his successes, but in Christian faith they accepted his gifts as an
evidence of the goodness of the Lord to them. The father cau-
tioned the young couple after one of their successful concerts:

"I hope you never let yourselves be carried away by all the
incense that has been burned before you of late, but that you
both gratefully give all the glory to God. For it is only through
Him that we can accomplish anything."

It should not be inferred that the remainder of Grieg's days
were unmixed successes. Indeed, there were few days that were
without some clouds. It seemed rather that each success must
be compensated for in an equal share of adversity. He had, to
begin with, a soaring, healthy spirit in a fragile body. His compositions were given unqualified endorsement by Liszt; he was
supported by leading Norwegian musical and literary lights,
such as Ibsen, Bjornson, Svendsen, and Nordraak; but his efforts to bring his fellow countrymen to a larger appreciation of
better music, and even of their own wealth of folk music, met
with a general attitude of self-complacency and indifference.

Grieg's meeting with Richard Nordraak proved a turning point in the life of the composer. They became acquainted at an opportune time, for Grieg had been debating how best to direct his genius to its fullest measure of efficiency. The two young men first met in Tivoli Park in Copenhagen, Denmark. Nordraak was also an able composer, and had to his credit the jubilant music of the Norwegian anthem. The two men had opposite natures. Whereas Grieg was modest and retiring, Nordraak possessed an enthusiasm that bordered on fanaticism for his beloved Norway. His contagious zeal was so effective that thenceforward the compass of Grieg's life pointed northward. Grieg acknowledged Nordraak's part in giving direction to the later years of his life, in these words: "I was longing to find expression for the best that was in me—a best that lay a thousand miles from Leipzig and its atmosphere; but that it lay in love of my fatherland and in my feeling for the great, melancholy, westland nature I did not know and would never perhaps have found out if I had not, through Nordraak, been led to self-examination. This had its first result in the *Humoresques, Opus 6,* dedicated to Nordraak, in which the direction of development is plainly shown."

The composer was led to dedicate his life to the cause of Norwegian music by reproducing Norway's life, scenery, and folklore in his creative works, by participating in Norwegian choral and orchestral performances, and by heroic efforts to establish musical institutions in Norway.

That the Norwegian Government appreciated his efforts is borne out by the stipend granted him when he was thirty, which enabled him to devote his energies entirely to creative work.

Two of Grieg's most important compositions were written while the composer was still a young man, the *Piano Concerto in A minor,* written when he was twenty-five and the *Peer Gynt* suites, begun when he was thirty. The Peer Gynt music is based on the dramatic play *Peer Gynt,* by Henrik Ibsen, Norwegian poet and dramatist. The music was written by Grieg at the request of Ibsen.

Peer Gynt unfolds the adventures of an irresolute Norwegian peasant youth, who, early in the play, startles his mother
Ase with his fantastic boasting. He attends, uninvited, a country
wedding, where Solvejg, despite his uncouth behavior, falls in
love with him. But Peer Gynt, always the rascal, runs away with
the beautiful bride Ingrid, only to desert her in the mountain
wildness. His escapades take him to the "Hall of the Mountain
King." He returns to his home and finds Ase on her deathbed.
He next turns up in Africa, which is the setting for Grieg's
"Arabian Dance," "Anitra's Dance," and "Morning." Peer, now
an old man, returns to Norway but suffers shipwreck on the
homeward voyage. When at last he reaches home he finds
Solvejg, a gray-haired old lady, still devoted, still faithful. He
sinks exhausted in her arms.

After spending a number of years in musical activities in
the Norwegian capital, the Griegs resided for a time at Loftus,
a little village on a branch of the Hardanger Fiord, where Norwegian nature smiles its sweetest. Choosing a secluded hillslope
to which there was no visible path, the composer built a little
hut, just large enough for a fireplace, a piano, and himself,
where he could find the solitude that was a necessary part of
his creative processes. But soon the curious eyes of neighboring peasants found his little retreat, and thereafter small groups
would gather near the windows, ready to witness the birth of
his brain children.

So he decided that he would move his "tune house" nearer
the fiord, to a spot that would be invulnerable to eye attacks.
Moving day became a neighborhood affair. The peasantry from
near and far were summoned to lend their aid to the removal of
the studio and witness to its dedication. Let us view the scene
in Grieg's inimitable description:

"One beautiful morning on the stroke of 9 the whole stout
company assembled, obviously in holiday mood, which was in
no way damped at sight of the numerous preparations in the way
of food and drink I had had the wisdom to lay in. A barrel of
Hardanger ale, of the kind known for its strength, stood ready

besides an adequate supply of genuine Norwegian aqua vitae, with appropriate edible delicacies, such as 'flatbrodlefser,' 'kringler' and so on. All these national delights were dispatched to the new site where, when the work was over, the actual feast was to take place. . . .

"Roles were assigned, each man ordered to his place, and it will be long before I forget that glorious moment in the history of the 'Compost' when, with a mighty tug, he was loosed from his foundations amidst the tumultuous shouts of applause from the assembled peasantry, while the pupils from the near-by girls' institute, who had established themselves outside their school in a body, rent the air with an enthusiastic hurrah, full of youth and spring, and accompanied by the waving of handkerchiefs. It was as if we were all electrified by these blithe, gay girl voices and with rejoicing the house was now borne off—sometimes dragged, sometimes rolled on the trunks of young trees— to its new home. . . . When at last the house was lifted onto its new foundation, where among birches and rowans by the glass-clear fiord, it looked superb, the bowls of ale began to circulate, and they were needed, for many a stout carl could be seen to wipe the sweat from his brow after the exertion."

In 1885 Grieg built a lovely villa on Nordass Lake, and named it Troldhaugen. There, together with his wife and her sister, he was to spend the remainder of his life. The house, with the Norsk flag proudly waving from its tower, was set high on a hill which sloped precipitously toward the fiord. On the shore the master had a little cabin-studio; near at hand his little fishing boat, rocked by the gentle waves, awaited his pleasure. Here, attuned to the heartstrings of nature, stirred by the rhythm of her pulsating life, his soul overflowed in ecstatic song. Many of his instrumental compositions, too, record his impressions gained in trysts with nature: "Autumn Overture," "To Spring," "Butterfly," "Birdling," "Evening in the Mountain," and others.

Grieg rates with Schubert and Franz as one of the greatest of song writers. His best songs are attributable to the ideal state of his married life, and were inspired by the mutual love between him and his companion. This lovely couple came to be esteemed during their lifetime, not only in Norway, but throughout the world. Their silver wedding at Troldhaugen was attended by nearly five thousand people. Early that morning the majestic strains of Luther's "A Mighty Fortress" rose from the garden as a prelude to the flux of guests and presents that were to press in during the day. Gifts of every description, from paintings and silverware to a Steinway piano, came in a steady stream from admirers and colleagues in Scandinavia and England. There was a lawn supper followed by a concert given by a large choir; there were intermittent cannon salutes accompanied by the glare of fireworks from the surrounding islands. To the little ailing master and his wife the occasion, so spontaneous and heartfelt, was unforgettable. It signified to them that spending his days, his lifeblood, for the uplift of his people had not been in vain; it was bringing to him the gratitude not alone of Norway but of the world.

Grieg may be said to be an artist in miniature. Because of ill-health, especially his asthmatic condition, it became increasingly difficult for him to work at long intervals, and this was why so many of his works are cast in a smaller mold. But these are so original and so national in character as to give him a place with the great individualists of musical history.

Grieg still lives in his music, in the minds of lovers of music everywhere, and especially, in the hearts of his countrymen. One Norwegian author, David Johansen, wrote of him: "He has stimulated the flow of blood in a people who were sickening because violence had been done to their natural functions. He has made it possible for the fresh blood to flow out once more from the heart through the whole organism."

Grieg gave Norway a place in the musical sun.

Edward MacDowell

1861-1908

A house of dreams untold,
It looks out over the whispering tree-tops
And faces the setting sun.—MacDowell.

〜

THIS "house of dreams" was not a medieval castle or an elegant mansion but a little log cabin, perched on the side of a wooded slope in a deep forest near Peterborough, New Hampshire. A sparkling spring gurgled merrily near by, a valley of forests lay below, and in the distance loomed Mount Monadnock.

The cabin was plainly furnished, with a cot, some tables and chairs, and a cozy fireplace. These were the simple appointments that satisfied the master for whom it was built, and here he sat and gazed out through the latticed windows and dreamed dreams.

The cabin itself was the realization of a dream. It was an escape from the vexations and petty grievances of humankind. It afforded an opportunity to live in the solitude and soul-cleansing atmosphere of nature, to restore depleted energies, and to hear the revivifying message of the wind.

The path to the door of the dream cabin—the path of the years—had been long and winding, now coursing through dif-

143

ficult mountain passes and now through fragrant flower beds or
by quiet streams.

Whereas that famous log cabin of an earlier day marked the
birthplace of the great American leader of men, Abraham Lincoln, the log cabin near Peterborough marked the later years,
the crowning achievements, of the great American master of
music—Edward MacDowell.

It was a far cry from the seclusion of Peterborough to the
bustle and clamor that was a part of New York City, even in the
days when Edward was born there. It was a far cry, too, from
the freedom of thought expressed here in poetry, music, and art
to the strict tenets and plain living of the Quaker persuasion of
his ancestors. Throughout his lifetime Edward could recollect
with ease the long sermonless, musicless Friends' meetings of
his boyhood. Many traits of his character, such as orderliness, love
of peace, and seriousness, were the fruitage of the teachings
of church and home.

Edward loved books and pictures and music despite the
fact that these things were discountenanced by the church as
smacking of worldliness. Edward's mother, who was not a
Quaker, was especially ambitious concerning the careers of her
three boys. She early visualized a brilliant career for Edward. She
did everything possible to encourage his various interests. She
bought him books on many topics and arranged for his music lessons when he was eight. It was necessary to break down considerable prejudice on the part of the Quaker side of the family.
"Music, will thee make a miserable musician of that boy?" pro-
tested Grandfather MacDowell. "He ought to be learning some
useful work. Music is not work. The only musician who works
is the hand organ man with a monkey. He at least turns a crank
for his money!" But in time Mrs. MacDowell won over all opposition.

Edward's first teacher was a native of South America. Although Edward thought highly of his teacher and loved his
music, he was not particularly fond of practicing. One day a
visitor at the MacDowell home heard amateurish thumpings,

that were anything but pianistic, coming from the music room. She opened the door to find Edward lying on the floor absorbed in reading a new book, while at the piano his brother Walter, bribed by two pennies, pounded out pretenses for the benefit of the other members of the family.

Edward's teacher counted among his friends Mme. Teresa Carreno, noted woman pianist. Juan Buitrago was eager to have her hear his new talented pupil play, and invited her, while she was his guest, to accompany him to the MacDowell home. She became very much interested in Edward, gave him music lessons for a time, and later did much to bring his music, especially his concertos, before the public.

By the time Edward was ten years old his frail body had developed to muscular proportions, and he was excelling in sports and games. Before he was eleven he had already won a prize in gun marksmanship.

The MacDowell boys generally spent their vacation on their uncle's farm near the Catskill Mountains. They tramped the wild woods; they fished in the mountain streams; they found rare flowers and came to know the habits and haunts of many creatures of the wild. In days to come Edward would recapture these nature jaunts of his youth in his tone pictures. His compositions would include moods inspired by waterside reveries of his childhood. One such, "The Brook," from *Four Little Poems* for piano, bears a carefree verse by Bulwer:

> "Gay below the cowslip bank, see the billow dances;
>   There I lay, beguiling time—when I liv'd romances:
>   Dropping pebbles in the wave, fancies into fancies."

His familiarity with birds and bird lore would be reflected in "The Eagle," a musical portrayal of Tennyson's lines:

> "He clasps the crag with crooked hands;
>   Close to the sun in lonely lands,
>   Ringed with the azure world, he stands.

"The wrinkled sea beneath him crawls;
He watches from his mountain walls,
And like a thunderbolt he falls."

He would humorously trace the revels of "Cottontails" in his "To Br'er Rabbit," and he would catch the spirit of the hunt in his "Wild Chase."

A new adventure was in store for Edward when he was twelve. His mother, realizing that the boy possessed more than ordinary potentialities, felt that he should early have the privilege of breathing the atmosphere of the Old World and of partaking of its broadening influence. The voyage was important in that it was a prelude to an extended stay in Europe, beginning when Edward was fifteen.

On his second trip to Europe he became a student at the Paris Conservatoire, where Debussy was also a student at the time. Along with his studies in piano and theory he was given private tutoring in French. During his lesson hour one day Edward drew a picture of his teacher, which the latter discovered just as the sketch was finished. He was so impressed with the likeness that he asked to keep it, later showing it to a famous French artist. The painter was even more impressed and offered Edward a three years' scholarship in painting. Mrs. MacDowell and Edward carefully considered the offer, but the call to the ministry of music was so clear and irresistible that they decided in favor of continuing his musical studies.

After several years in Paris, Edward went to Germany, studying first at Stuttgart and then at Frankfurt, where he studied under Raff, Swiss composer and a former pupil of Liszt. Raff was generously encouraging to his young American pupil, and it was largely through this master that Edward found the key to the creative treasures of his own mind. At nineteen the earliest of these treasures was given to the world in his *First Modern Suite* for piano.

Raff also assisted Edward by sending piano pupils to him. Among these pupils was a Connecticut girl, Miss Marian Nevins.

She seemed reluctant at first to study with an American when she had come to Germany in order to study with a European teacher; but under Raff's persuasion she yielded and made excellent progress under MacDowell's tutorship.

Several years of hard work toward a common goal followed, during which teacher and pupil found that their similar ideals and aspirations had drawn about them a bond that led from the Dorian and Phrygian modes to the sweet concord of love. They began to plan their future together on a foundation of high idealism. She would go on first to America, and when Edward reached the age of twenty-three he would return to the States, and they would marry.

Meanwhile the "handsome American" stayed on in Europe, busily engaged in teaching, composing, and delving into the poetry and lore of England, France, and Germany, and fitting himself for his chosen calling. Edward MacDowell was a fine representative of American manhood. He was tall, ruddy, with blue eyes, dark hair, and already at eighteen he displayed a red and pointed mustache. He possessed a remarkably wide range of artistic and athletic aptitudes. "He loved," wrote James Huneker, "a fast and furious boxing match. The call of his soul won him for music and poetry. Otherwise he would have been a sea-captain, a soldier or an explorer in far-away countries. He had the physique, he had the big, manly spirit."

When MacDowell completed his *First Concerto for Piano*, it so pleased Raff that he suggested that he take it to Liszt for his appraisal. MacDowell, eager for the blessing of the reigning musical monarch, set out for Weimar, with his manuscript under his arm. He began the pilgrimage with all the courage of a crusader, but when he reached the building in which the master had his studio, his gallantry vanished. He waited while others came and went. He entered the vestibule and waited again. Finally, when news was brought to Liszt about the young man, the grand old master came out and, in his friendly manner, read Raff's letter of introduction and invited MacDowell inside. The concerto was arranged for two pianos, so MacDowell played the solo part and Eugen d'Albert, famous pianist who was present, played the orchestral parts. Liszt commended the work highly and turning to D'Albert, admonishingly said, "You must bestir yourself if you do not want to be outdone by our young American." Liszt's sanction of his art gave MacDowell a new sense of confidence in his creative ability.

In the month of June, 1884, the composer came to America and was married to Miss Nevins at her home in Connecticut. They returned to Europe, living for a time in England, in Switzerland, and in Germany. Wherever they made their home, although modest in its furnishings, it was a home where joy reigned, where peace abode. It was a home that knew the companionship of books, the luxury of flowers, the charm of music. It was a home of mutual aims and ideals. It was a home that was prepared to withstand any test of hardship or sacrifice that might arise to thwart their plans for fuller musical service. In London, where the couple resided for a time in pursuit of further knowledge along orchestral lines, their funds ran low. Rather than cut short their stay and deprive the composer of this necessary study and stimulus, Mrs. MacDowell sold her family silver, and thus enabled him to complete an important phase of his artistic development.

A year after their marriage the MacDowells moved to a little fairylike cottage near Wiesbaden, Germany. Here, at the edge of a forest, they lived for several years. In this serene and picturesque environment the composer's most fruitful creative period began. During his stay at Wiesbaden he completed his compositions from Opus 23 through Opus 35. This series includes his brilliant *Second Concerto in D minor* for piano and orchestra, which has become standard repertory with pianists, also the symphonic poem *Lancelot and Elaine,* as well as the songs *From an Old Garden* and *Four Little Poems,* Opus 32, for piano. In both these sets the composer's predilection for the poetry and music of nature is manifest.

As MacDowell's creative outpourings increased, his fellow Americans became aware of the certainty of his artistic future.

The feeling grew that his endowments and influence could best serve the future of American music if he resided on American soil. With this end in view some of his admirers made a path to his door and urged that he return to his native land. So in 1888 the composer and his wife returned to America, where, in time, they were to see the name of MacDowell established as one of the greatest names in the history of American music.

Their homeward voyage stirred again the composer's fertile imagination in response to the spell of the sea. His *Sea Pieces*, Opus 55, commemorates his voyages in eloquent tone pictures of moods evoked by the vastness and awesome mystery of the ocean. The first of these seascapes, "To the Sea," introduced by the dedication, "Ocean, Thou Mighty Monster," "for breadth of conception and concentrated vividness of effect is not excelled in the contemporary literature of the piano," according to Lawrence Gilman, music critic. And it is the more remarkable in that this is accomplished within the limits of two pages.

MacDowell proceeds from one episode of the voyage to another throughout the eight numbers in the suite. He records his impression of the myriads of stars at night in his tender "Starlight," with an original quatrain:

> "The stars are but the chorus,
> That sing around the throne
> Of grey old Ocean's spouse,
> The Moon's pale majesty."

He writes of his first glimpse of an iceberg in "From a Wandering Iceberg":

> "An errant Princess of the North,
> A virgin snowy white,
> Sails down the summer seas,
> To realms of burning light."

He relives the voyage of the Pilgrims on the *Mayflower* in his "A.D. 1620":

> "The yellow setting sun
> Melts the lazy sea to gold,
> And gilds the swaying galleon
> That forward to a land of promise
> Lunges hugely on."

That a profound sense of awe and of man's littleness overwhelmed him when the steamer had been at sea for several days is evident in the inscription and music of the eighth number, "In Mid Ocean":

> "Inexorable!
> Thou straight line of eternal fate
> That ringest the world.
> While on the moaning breast
> We play our puny parts,
> And reckon us immortal."

The MacDowells spent eight years in Boston, where he was engaged in teaching, concertizing, and composing. In 1896 the course of his career branched in two directions, northward and southward. In that year he was given the professorship in the department of music at Columbia University, which position he held for eight years. Some of his important lectures have been published in his book *Critical and Historical Essays*. MacDowell undertook this phase of his career with his usual devotion and painstaking thoroughness, insomuch, that his health suffered irreparably under the burdens of his arduous duties at the university, together with the demands imposed by his unrelenting creative urges.

The north branch meandered through Maine to the seacoast and then inland to the hills of New Hampshire, finally settling in a deserted farmhouse near Peterborough. This, thought the composer, would make an ideal retreat from the workaday world, where the broken strings of his overworked soul and body could be mended and tuned again to respond to nature's improvisations. The farm was purchased, and the rambling house on the hill was christened Hillcrest. A little farther into the woods the log cabin, his "house of dreams," was built. The cabin became the birthplace of many of his best musical thoughts. Here he could look into the heart of a flower, make friends with the denizens of the forest, or penetrate into the deep woods and then express his idyls in music.

The rare personality of the man is reflected in the simplicity of his joys. He fled from artificiality to the pure and natural pleasures to be found in walking in a garden or breathing the fresh scent of the pine trees. A glance at the titles in any of his piano volumes, such as the *Woodland Sketches* or the *New England Idyls,* will reveal the master's enthusiasm for things of the natural world. "His music is redolent of the breath and odour of woodland places," wrote Lawrence Gilman, "of lanes and moors and gardens; or it is saturated with salt spray; or it communicates the incommunicable in its voicing of that indefinable enchantment of association which clings about certain aspects, certain phases of the visible world—that subtle emotion of things past and irrecoverable which may inhabit a field at night, or a quiet street at dusk, or a sudden intimation of spring in the scent of lilacs."

Within the covers of the composer's albums a veritable tonal panorama of natural scenes is brought to view. There are seasonal scenes illustrated by "Mid-Summer," "Mid-Winter," and "The Joy of Autumn," from his *New England Idyls.* There are elegant flower scenes such as "To a Water-Lily" from the *Woodland Sketches,* "An Old Garden," and "With Sweet Lavender," both from the *New England Idyls.* There are broad views, impressive and stately, such as, "In Deep Woods," whose inspiration is indicated in a four-line motto:

> "Above, long slender shafts of opal flame,
> Below, the dim cathedral aisles;
> The silent mystery of immortal things
> Broods o'er the woods at eve."

"From a German Forest," the third of the *Fireside Tales,* reveals the tenor of the composer's style and illustrates his musical inventiveness in portraying natural settings and moods.

His marked originality is stamped on every score. It is particularly
evident in the last ten measures, a *codetta* of kaleidoscopic transi-
tions that is delightfully suggestive in its plaintive appeal as the
music of the woods resolves into one lone voice, like a faint
echo dying away in the far distance.

MacDowell's compositions, in addition to those having their
inspiration in nature, consist of numerous musical reflections
which indicate his fascination for history and legend. His *Indian
Suite* for orchestra reveals his knowledge of the customs and
melodies of the North American Indians. His *Sonata Eroica*,
for piano, is based on the Arthurian legends of old England. In
his *Keltic Sonata* he has revived the "stupendous passions and
aspirations of bards and heroes and sublime adventures of the
ancient Celts. The *Norse Sonata,* dedicated to Edvard Grieg,
glorifies the intrepid spirit of the Norse Vikings.

MacDowell's complete works range from his piano miniatures through the highest classical forms exemplified in his four-
piano sonatas, two-piano concertos, and several suites. His compositions are the musical autobiography of a typical American.
Accompanied by mottoes in original and quoted verse, they are
true stories of his life, abounding in adventure and history,
tragedy and joy, love and drama. He tells of his visits to the
Old World: to Germany in pieces based on lines of Goethe
and Heine, and in his partial adoption of the German romantic
style; to Scotland in his Scotch poem "Far Away on the Rock-
Coast of Scotland," and in his *Keltic Sonata*. Whether at home
or abroad he had the rare faculty, first, of seeing new beauties
and discovering new truths in familiar things, and then of
transcribing these revelations into music.

The individuality of MacDowell is especially apparent in
his felicity as a tone painter of his impressions of things past and
present. He was able to capture in music the freshness of a
fleeting moment of gladsome fruition or of an engaging re-
miniscence. His musical portrayals speak eloquently of his aware-
ness of life's true purposes and designs. His sensitive style, depicted in delicate melodic hues or in vivid dashes of harmonic

color, flowered into lasting musical creations that have helped to fill, with honor, America's niche in the hall of musical fame.

The piano was the vehicle of expression most frequently used by the composer. It was his first love. Even his smaller piano compositions reveal his singularly poetic imagination, his romantic-impressionistic tendencies, his whimsical humor, his distaste for the commonplace. They reveal him as a musical master of condensation.

Though MacDowell has no symphony to his credit, he often chose the symphonic poem as a further channel through which to direct the flow of his creative thinking. Lastly, it was but natural that MacDowell's genius for melody should destine him for a coveted place among song composers. In his book *Songs and Song Writers,* H. Fink rates MacDowell as one of the "Big Four" among song writers, in company with Schubert, Franz, and Grieg. Although the number of the American master's songs is small in comparison with those of the other first-rate song composers, they maintain a consistently high standard of excellence. Some are considered among the best in song literature.

The idea of the "dream house" had proved itself of such value as a stimulus to the master's creative impulses that the Mac-Dowells began to think of expanding its usefulness. Why not give other creative minds the advantages of the seclusion and inspiration afforded by such an ideal setting as that of the log cabin? So, in time, the log cabin became the nucleus of a growing group of isolated studios, some of which are replicas of shrines and important buildings in other parts of the world. One of these, the John Alexander Memorial, is considered one of the most beautiful small buildings in America. Although each building has its own individual design, a quiet rustic atmosphere pervades the entire colony. Beginning with about sixty acres, the MacDowell Colony now covers six hundred acres, and maintains about twenty-four studios available to artists of proved talent.

In company with relatives living in New Hampshire, it was my pleasure to visit the colony in the autumn of 1944. After

reaching the outskirts of Peterborough, we found it necessary
to do a little searching to find the side road that led up to Hillcrest, for Nature had done her best to hide the retreat in dense
foliage. We were immediately impressed, on reaching the "island
in a sea of trees," by the quiet, friendly atmosphere all about
Hillcrest, typified, it seemed, in the welcome of the low swing-
ing gate. Just beyond the house the hill slopes gracefully into the
old garden, where hollyhocks, like erect sentinels, stand guard
over a host of variegated flowers. A grape arbor, rare shrubs, and
a sundial add a somber touch to the scenic spot.

Here and there along the winding lanes leading into the
woods, isolated studios dot the rolling landscape. In the seclusion
of these natural settings workers in the arts pursue their particular
fields of specialization unmolested. The colony, unique both as
to plan and operation, is the complete answer to a creator's
dream, whether he be painter, poet, writer, sculptor, or composer.

We paused at the "dream house." Its music was stilled. It
stood a weather-beaten reminder of the happy days when the
young couple gave themselves to the furtherance of noble ideals.
It is indeed a humble monument compared with the buildings,
statues, and obelisks that have been erected to the memories of
some men. But MacDowell needed no memorial of granite or
stone to perpetuate his name. His memory is hallowed in living
monuments. His contributions toward the betterment of mankind are remembered, not in material things, but in things of
the spirit.

As we entered the low-ceilinged living room of Hillcrest,
Mrs. MacDowell, gracious and mentally alert despite her eighty-
six years, was just descending the stairway leading to the parlor.
Her quiet, unassuming manner seemed to blend with the tranquil, meditative atmosphere of the room. As she talked of music
of the present, one's eyes played truant to catch glimpses of the
book-lined walls, of the bronze bust of the composer, and of his
grand piano. One's mind, too, kept reverting to the past and to
the important role our hostess had played in fostering the ideals

of the colony, and earlier as a never-failing source of inspiration to the master.

In fancy we leave the immediate present to leaf through the pages of Hillcrest's history, back to its earliest days. And lo! some of the pages come alive with the expectancy of wishful planning as the youthful couple launch their career. Some pages are laden with the satisfaction of achievements attained. A few pages are tear-stained as the struggle with adversity became almost overwhelming. Nearly every page breathes courage and strength of purpose. Interesting incidents in their life experiences are unfolded in many chapters, throwing light on the background of compositions that have come to be loved the world over.

One story found in an early chapter reveals how the preservation of some of the master's works was due to the care and resourcefulness of Mrs. MacDowell. On pages yellow with age we are able to make out the details of the incident as it happened a half century ago:

One evening, soon after the composer had left his music study, Mrs. MacDowell entered the room to replace books and manuscripts in readiness for the work of a new day. As she busied herself about the room, a crumpled piece of music paper on the hearth attracted her eye. Knowing her husband's habit of discarding anything that was not up to his usual high standard, she smoothed out the wrinkled sheet. As she hummed through the theme scrawled on the discarded paper, she was immediately impressed that she held in her hand a musical gem, small but precious.

The following morning as the composer was about to retire to his study, Mrs. MacDowell gave him the slip of manuscript paper, suggesting that the theme he had written the preceding day was too promising to discard. Mr. MacDowell went to the piano and again played over the short melody. In the light of a new day the theme took on a new luster; it showed fresh possibilities. The master too decided that possibly the little musical jewel was genuine. So in his musical workshop the motive took shape under the cunning of his craftmanship. It was refined and polished.

Again it was brought to the light, finished in every detail. As the MacDowells scrutinized the completed work, there was, likely, a grateful twinkle in Mrs. MacDowell's eyes as she thought of the wrinkled sheet and the hearth fire.

In the gentle strains of the little tone-poem the composer had couched an appeal as simple and direct as its chosen name-sake, the rose. Although MacDowell steadfastly averred that he regarded "To a Wild Rose" as just a "still small voice" in music, could he have looked down through the years, he would have discovered the perpetual freshness of its dulcet tones being wafted to earth's remotest parts.

For more than a decade the congenial atmosphere about Hillcrest proved a rich blessing to the composer. In his summer and midwinter visits he could partake of the delightful changing moods yielded in the contentment and cheer of the hearth glow, or in the exhilarating zest of a crisp snowfall, or in the solemn solitude of the forest at twilight. These refreshing sojourns were as sustenance to his soul and as a whetstone to his imagination. From his natural retreat there went out to the world such messages of courage and peace as are found only in living music.

The master was busy—so busy, dreaming, planning, working. Then, almost imperceptibly, there came the realization to those close to him that the strings of his instrument—the same instrument that had been attuned to every shade of musical color—were losing their resiliency until they no longer responded even to the touch of the one who had been its greatest inspiration. Then, its usefulness impaired, the instrument soon gave way under the strain.

The master was buried near the log cabin. Inscribed on a bronze plaque set in the boulder marking his grave are the lines:

> "A house of dreams untold,
> It looks out over the whispering tree-tops
> And faces the setting sun."

Claude Debussy

1862-1918

*To rid music of the legacy of clumsy,
falsely interpreted traditions.*—DEBUSSY.

⁓

THROUGH the cycles of the ages music, language of heaven and earth, has ministered to the spiritual and physical needs of mankind. The importance of music in the experience of Israel is evident in the large number of musicians directly engaged in the devotional services. There were reputedly four thousand voices trained in the antiphonal singing of the psalms during the reign of King David. King Solomon, according to Josephus, treasured forty thousand harps and psalteries and two hundred thousand silver trumpets to enhance the solemnity and beauty of the temple worship.

A Biblical instance of music as a therapeutic benefactor is recorded during the turbulent days when King Saul placed David's life in jeopardy. "And it came to pass, when the evil spirit from God was upon Saul, that David took an harp, and played with his hand: so Saul was refreshed, and was well, and the evil spirit departed from him." Modern research continues to reveal new aspects of music's properties in bringing beneficial responses to the mind of man, and subsequently to his body. Shakespeare recognized this power in music. In "A Song to the Lute in Music" he mused:

"O heavenly gift that rules the mind,
E'en as the stern doth rule the ship!
O music, whom the gods assigned
To comfort man, whom cares would nip!
Since thou both man and beast doth move,
What beast is he will thee disprove?"

One of the most potent blessings that music brings to mankind lies in its efficacy as a promoter of good will. It breathes friendliness. It brings understanding and unity among nations. It knows no color, race, or caste. It speaks one language, the language of the heart.

"Forever old, forever young,
Immortal Music Voice Divine,
Heard clearly, purely, here among
All tongues—thou Universal Tongue—
Since morning stars together sung
Our souls are one with thine!"
—JAMES WHITCOMB RILEY.

As if in gratitude for the blessings it bestows, men and nations have in return given to the art of music the masterworks and perfected musical instruments which make up its rich and varied heritage. Prominent among the nations that have contributed to the art stands France, from the days when the troubadours roamed the vine-covered hills in Provence during the Middle Ages to the ultramodern composers of today. She has contributed outstanding men in the operatic field, men such as Bizet and Gounod and Massenet; oratorio and instrumental composers such as Berlioz and Franck; high-ranking organ composers like Widor, Guilmant, and Vierne.

Among the moderns Debussy, leader of the impressionists, has enriched the musical art with resources that have placed a new mold on creative thinking. His vision and tenacity of purpose have opened the doors into the inner chambers of the citadel of music.

Claude Achille Debussy was the son of a china dealer in Saint Germain-en-Laye, France. The setting of his birthplace was ideal in its natural surroundings, a countryside of gardens, orchards, and forests; and in its associations with important events of the past. Louis XIV was among its native sons. There was little danger, however, that the little village would lose itself in its past or in isolation, for within sight rose the skyline of Paris. Claude's unpropitious boyhood was begun over his father's little china shop, on a narrow, cobblestone market street. Neither of his parents was musical. They had wished that their son would follow a naval career, but if Claude envisioned himself sailing down the sea lanes, every vessel on the water assumed the shape of a musical barque. His parents were poor. On the other hand, Claude had aristocratic tastes. He was fond of delicate art objects, etchings, carved animals, and rare pictures; but it was often difficult to reconcile a rich lad's tastes with a poor lad's purse. This penchant for delicately wrought workmanship manifested itself later in the exquisite finish of his compositions.

An aunt on his mother's side started Claude on the road to musical joy and glory. By the time he was eleven he was a student at the Paris Conservatoire, where he remained for eleven years, obtaining prizes in *solfege,* piano playing, accompanying, counterpoint, and fugue, and finally the coveted Grand Prix de Rome.

While Claude was still a student, an opportunity to put his music into service came in the form of an invitation for him to spend the summer with a wealthy Russian family vacationing in Switzerland. Claude was to teach piano to the two boys and serve as pianist and accompanist in the family musicales that took place in the evenings. Though he was only eighteen, his work so pleased his hostess, Mme. von Meck (Tchaikovsky's patroness) that she paid him handsomely for his summer's work and promised subsequent engagements, which, when they materialized, gave impetus to his careeer.

The third time that Claude sojourned with the Von Mecks they were living at their sumptuous residence in Moscow. This visit was important to the young Frenchman, because he then became acquainted with exponents of the Russian school, with names such as Tchaikovsky, Borodin, Rimski-Korsakov, and Musorgski. He imbibed the Oriental atmosphere of their music and became acquainted with the whole tone scale that some of these composers were using.

Another youthful impression that affected his musical style was gained while he served in the French army. When he heard the sound of the camp bugle and also the bells from a near-by convent, he was fascinated by the resonance of the bugle and bells, and their accompanying overtones. He delved further into the principles of harmonics, in which fundamental tones vibrate as a whole and in parts. He then based the harmonies and coloring of his compositions on these natural laws of tone, which resulted in a new, rich, and varied texture.

Still another influence on Debussy's art was his delight in nature. He has left us word pictures as well as musical pictures of his tender response toward nature's voice. He said, "I lingered late one autumn evening in the country, irresistibly fascinated by the magic of old world forests. From yellowing leaves, fluttering earthward, celebrating the glorious agony of the trees, from the clangorous angelus bidding the fields to slumber, rose a sweet persuasive voice, counseling perfect oblivion. The sun was setting solitary. Beasts and men turned peacefully homeward, having accomplished their impersonal tasks."

The titles of many of the compositions that came from his pen indicate the importance of nature as a background for his music. These are a few: "The Wind on the Plains," "Clouds," "Reflections in the Water," "The Little Shepherd," and "Gardens in the Rain." In evaluating Debussy's contribution to musical literature, Maurice Dumesnil emphasizes its natural background in these words: "To love it best one must also be a lover of nature, of deep forests, of medieval legends which tell of old castles, of ancient walls worn by time and covered with ivy; one must have felt the spell of the declining sun on seashores and river bends, and perceived in an autumn park the exalted fragrance of dying flowers."

Debussy won the Prix de Rome for his cantata *The Prodigal Child*. For many weeks prior to the examinations the contestants worked on their respective compositions in the confinement of the loge, quarters for prize aspirants. Debussy had tacked up a tape measure marking off the number of days until the contest piece should be submitted. A portion was then clipped from the measure each day as the deadline approached; thus he prodded himself to finish his cantata on time. It also served as a reminder that the drudgery would soon be at an end. How he despised such clock inspiration!

When Debussy received the news that the judges had given him the prize he showed a surprising lack of elation. He had tried and tried hard to win the award, but now that it was his own, the realization dawned on him that it meant his musical freedom would be circumscribed, his musical independence jeopardized. Even in his youth Debussy was not of the ordinary run of men or musicians, either temperamentally or artistically. He had accepted the creed of Musorgski, that "musicians should not base their art on the laws of the past, but on the needs of the future."

In contrast with the youth's nonchalant attitude toward his scholarship was the general jubilation it created among his parents and friends. During the days before leaving for Rome, Claude rode high on the crest of an unusual solicitude toward him on the part of all within his friendly circle. These days reveal unerringly, on the other hand, that the Debussys did not ride on a high tide of finance. One holiday Claude decided he would spend the day visiting some dear friends. He donned his new black suit, and inasmuch as it was a very special occasion, anticipated wearing the beautiful watch he had received as a parting present from Mme. von Meck. The gift had been tucked away in a box in a corner of the cupboard. Claude's anticipation suddenly turned to dismay, for as he looked into the box he was startled to find that the watch was gone. Father Debussy, red-faced and stammering, then confessed that he had pawned the watch in order to relieve a strain in the family budget.

11

When Claude boarded the train for Rome he was surrounded by a miscellaneous assortment of packages, baggage, and trunks. In his proud possession was the watch, for which the redemption price had been paid. He sat near the window, enjoying to the full the panorama of vineyards, cypress trees, and orange blossoms as the train roared on toward Rome.

The city of Rome, for all its wealth of art and tradition, and its opportunity for study, failed to appeal to the young Frenchman. The villa where he resided became to him an "Etruscan tomb." He thought of every conceivable excuse to visit Paris, and managed, by circumvention, to make several such trips. Long before his three-year tenure had expired, he permanently left the institution. Claude was of such an independent and individual nature that he was unable to "do as the Romans do." He carried home with him very little that he cared to hold in happy remembrance of Rome outside of his meetings with some great men in music, including Verdi, Sgambati, and Liszt.

Now that his apprenticeship was coming to a close, Claude settled down to the serious business of carving a career. He took a job with a publishing firm at seventy dollars a month. He increased his income a little by means of odd jobs, such as teaching and accompanying. This enabled him to maintain a little apartment. He was able to save sufficient funds to visit the capitals of England and Austria. In Vienna he met Johannes Brahms, who shocked Claude's French sensibility by his unkempt person and unpredictable manners.

As Debussy's career progressed, his departure from the conventional became more pronounced. He was not content with following the musical paths already laid out by earlier masters. He chose to blaze a new trail in untried color possibilities and in greater freedom of expression. He had revolutionary ideas. "I shall never coop up my musical ideas within the cell structures of the old models," were his own words. "I shall give them space, freedom, life."

The art of Debussy is, above all else, highly individual. His compositions are the mood impressions of a musical dreamer—

subtle, nebulous, and often mysterious. They are characterized by "snippets of melody, . . . Oriental atmosphere, . . . vague rhythms, . . . shifting harmonies, . . . rare delicacy in taste. Daniel G. Mason aptly referred to the Debussy style with the three adjectives "vague, floating, kaleidoscopic."

Though village bred and a lover of the "City of Lights," Debussy continued to find his greatest inspiration in the wonders and suggestive moods of nature. "He has felt the haunting spell of her wayward beauty, and has transmitted some of her loveliness into sound. His quick sensibility enables him to seize the most delicate effects of light and shade, and he has rendered his art a plastic medium for recording fleeting impressions and fugitive glimpses."

The orchestral prelude *The Afternoon of a Faun,* completed by Debussy when he was about thirty-two, has been called "one of the major miracles of musical history." It crystallizes the master's distinctive style in its ever-changing harmonic coloring, its delicate choice of orchestral timbre, and its fantastic atmosphere. The prelude is based on a poem by Stephane Mallarme, and according to the composer, seeks to evoke the "successive scenes in which the longings and desires of the faun pass in the heat of the afternoon."

The three nocturnes for orchestra further reveal the musical personality of the composer in their exaltation of nature, in their sensual appeal, and in their deft artistry as mood pictures. *Clouds,* the first of the nocturnes, had its impetus as the composer crossed the bridge of La Concorde, and watched the "gray clouds drifting endlessly among gusts of raw wind," and heard the horn of a tug blowing "hoarsely on the Seine." The second nocturne, *Festivals,* more brilliant and vivid, represents "the restless dancing rhythms of the atmosphere, interspersed with abrupt scintillations." Other important works include the more formal *La Mer,* depicting three different aspects of the sea, and *Images,* a digression into the realm of reality. In the field of chamber music the *Quartet in G minor* remains his outstanding contribution. In dramatic style the opera *Pelleas et Melisande,* called, "a slow condensation of dreams," represents a decade of labor.

Pianists, in particular, have benefited in a large way from Debussy's pen. In creating an extensive repertory of piano compositions, the composer has created, moreover, a new style of interpretation. His works demand a sensitive touch, a dexterous use of the pedal, and a keen grasp of the atmospheric mood. His library for the piano includes many sets of pieces, such as the *Suite Bergamesque, Suite Pour Le Piano,* two sets of *Images,* the popular *Children's Corner,* two books of preludes, and two books of etudes.

The Children's Corner records some light and tender moments in the life of the composer. The suite was dedicated to his daughter, Claude-Emma when she was about four years old, and bears the inscription: "To my dearest Chou-Chou, with her father's affectionate apologies for what follows." Childish delights and fancies, with here and there a bit of mimicry, are sketched with elegant imagination in these picturesque miniatures. In "Doctor Gradus ad Parnassum" the composer enjoys a little musical fun-making at the expense of the technical etude writers, notably Clementi. "Jimbo's Lullaby" lulls to sleep Chou-Chou's stuffed toy elephant. The popular "Golliwogg's Cakewalk," a crisp, hilarious dance, with its rhythmic origin in the American cakewalk, brings the suite to a joyous close.

Debussy's songs, numbering over fifty, likewise are stamped with the individuality and finesse of his art. The French master's biographer, Oscar Thompson, says, "The essence of Debussy's musical personality is in the songs and they exhibit virtually every facet of his art. There is nothing like them in song literature."

Debussy combined with his dreams a doggedly persevering attitude toward the perfection of his ideals and a frankness of appraisal toward any work of art, whether it was his own or that of another. In regard to the publication of his *Reverie,* he wrote deprecatingly to the publishers:

"I regret very much your decision to publish the *Reverie.* . . . I wrote it in a hurry years ago, purely for material considerations. It is a work of no consequence and I frankly consider it absolutely no good." But the world remembers Debussy largely through his *Reverie* and *Clair de lune,* although these are not to be compared with his later creations.

Under the pen name of "Interviews with Mr. Eighth Note," Debussy digressed for a time into the journalistic field. His precise criticisms and witticisms were vivid, often caustic, and always picturesque. His comments on the music of Grieg exemplifies his style. Grieg's music gave him, he wrote, "the charming and bizarre sensation of eating a pink bonbon stuffed with snow."

In common with most pioneers Debussy suffered ridicule and pessimistic criticism for his departure from established methods and for his championing of artistic liberty. Slowly, as the smoke of misunderstanding has cleared, and the consuming fire of criticism has died out in darkness, there has emerged in the clear blue of world opinion, unsinged and lustrous, the genuineness of his worth.

When the calamity of war struck France in August, 1914, a pall, black and heavy, settled over the composer's life. Already the signs of his fatal illness were evident. The outlook was dark. He stood as one fixed between two scourges, outward and inward. For a time his creative urge was stifled as he saw the sons of France sacrificed in their heroic efforts to suppress tyranny. But as the war raged on, he came to realize that his part in maintaining the liberty of France lay in the messages of his music. Rallying his strength and morale, he caught again the reins of inspiration and diligent work.

Among his creations of this period Debussy wrote the words and music of the song "The Christmas of the Homeless Children." It was written in the winter of 1915, and expressed rather naively the heart pangs of the master as he was moved by the plight of the French refugee children:

> "They have wrecked my house,
> My brothers are dead.
> They have broken my doll,
> They have stolen my bed."

On and on, the two scourges, war and disease, relentlessly beat their destructive paths. For three years longer they spent their fury, with the composer one of the hapless victims. The year that closed the first world war, and stayed the threat to France's liberty, silenced also the voice of Claude Debussy, lover of musical freedom.

It is 1918. A lonely procession winds slowly down the Paris streets. Behind the hearse walk less than a score of mourners. The streets otherwise are well-nigh deserted, for the last German offensive is in progress. The eyes of the curious, bivouacked along the line of march, furtively follow the funeral procession. A whisper passes from one to another: *"The master is dead."*

Silently, except for the rumble of the approaching bombardment, Claude Debussy passes into the distance to the garden of peace.

The world since has been building a monument to his honor, a monument built out of a universal acceptance of his music. It is dedicated to the integrity, the idealism, the originality, of his musical art.

Ignace Jan Paderewski

1860-1941

*"His conscience will be his law, and each one
of his actions will be as clean as a sword
drawn from its sheath, shining in the sun."*

◜◞

SOME of the most inspirational chapters in the history
of music have been written during recent years. Since the turn
of the century scores of men and women of musical might have
risen to stellar heights of artistic achievement. The majority of
these have pursued their careers to varying degrees of fame and
fortune. A few, counting their accomplishments as incidental to
a higher goal, have sacrificed personal ambitions to devote their
gifts and means to the cause of humanity.

In the forefront of the music masters, whose art has been
spent in service for others, towers the distinguished figure of the
Polish patriot Ignace Jan Paderewski. His rare personality combined the endowments of genius with the simple virtues that
make up a noble character. He was not only a great musician; he
was a great man.

The morning of Paderewski's life was overcast with the dark
clouds of servitude that hung over the Polish people. As he
reached the afternoon of his experience, the sunlight of emancipa-
tion broke through and severed the bonds of slavery. But again

in its evening an ominous pall gathered that threw the country into the darkness of subjection once more.

Ignace was born in a little country village, Kurylowka, in Podolia, a province of old Poland. The rich soil of the countryside nourished fruit orchards in abundance. The air was fragrant with the smell of fresh fruit, and soft breezes played over a landscape of luxuriant verdure.

But there was a blight on the land in the form of an adversary, a three-headed monster, that was crushing out the spirit of the Polish people. There were blighted hopes too in the Paderewski home, for soon after Ignace's birth his mother died. So, on Ignace's father rested the sole responsibility of guiding the lives of his talented children while earning a livelihood as an administrator of estates. He sought to inculcate a sense of justice and of conscientious duty in the minds of Ignace and his sister, Antonina.

In the revolution of 1863, when Ignace was three, the Cossacks stormed the little village to quell the protests against the conscription of Poles into the Russian army. Suddenly a large company of Cossacks surrounded the Paderewski home to search the house for arms and propaganda material and to take the father a prisoner. In his *Memoirs,* Paderewski recalled the incident in these words:

"When the Cossacks first surrounded the house, I felt that something terrible was going to happen; but when they entered the house, then I knew that it was for my father they had come. I realized the danger. So I ran again to the tallest of the Cossacks, frightened as I was, and cried, 'What is happening to my father?' But he never answered or even looked at me. But I insisted and I kept on asking, as a child will, what had happened—why they were taking my father away, and if he would soon be back again. And then, the tall Cossack laughed, threw back his head and again gave me several very heavy strokes with the knout." Before the Cossacks retired from Kurylowka they killed many of the inhabitants and burned the village.

Shortly before the father's imprisonment he had arranged for

music lessons for the boy. He had taken notice of Ignace's craving for music, having watched him as he, with one finger, found
little melodies on the piano. His first teacher, a violinist, was
entirely lacking in a knowledge of the essentials of piano peda-
gogy, but he at least gave impetus to the musical inclinations of
Ignace and his sister by having them play duets. Sometimes the
performances became more "acrobatic than musical," and were
often accompanied by elbow fights and side kicks.

During the father's exile, which lasted a year, the children
lived with an aunt, and it was necessary to procure a new teacher.
He proved to be as incompetent as their former instructor. Even
at ten, considered late in the career of a concert artist, Ignace
was without a knowledge of the fundamental principles of piano
playing, especially regarding hand position and fingering.

In spite of these handicaps of his early life Ignace seemed
destined to succeed. He early set several goals for himself: he
hoped to reach a high degree of success in the field of music;
and he determined in some way to be of service to his country.
In rich measure he was to realize these goals.

Ignace first played in a charity concert when he was twelve.
Concerts in other places followed, until his talents came to the
attention of several influential families, who undertook to educate
him. Inasmuch as the boy had not yet had the privilege of
hearing any concerts of good music, either solo or orchestral, he
was given an invitation to visit Kiev during the winter season,
where he received a "tremendous impression" of several artists in
concert, and a new world opened before him.

On the return home their trip, made in two sleighs, almost
ended disastrously. The boy lay on the floor of the sleigh, covered
with a robe. He had no sooner fallen asleep than he was awak-
ened by the howling of a pack of wolves. Everyone was frightened. The horses trembled as the shrill cries of the ravenous
animals rent the air. One member of the party had a gun, but
one gun would have little effect on a whole pack. It was quickly
decided to load everything onto one sleigh and burn the other,
and thus frighten off the wolves. Fortunately, there were stacks

of straw still on the fields from the harvest. Fire was set to these. It was necessary to remain in the vicinity of these fires throughout the night to ward off the wolves until the party could pursue their journey by light of day.

Ignace's life adventure had begun. The father's decision that his boy should have a musical education coincided with the completion of the new railroad between Warsaw and their village. Aboard the first train to make the run, father and son rode to Warsaw and the great unknown.

After he had been registered at the Conservatory, lodging for Ignace was procured with a family having ten children. The home, a part of a piano warehouse, was simply furnished but aglow with the warmth of human kindness. The new environ- ment brought a happy change into the boy's life with so many new brothers and sisters to satisfy his love of company. He was delighted also with some of the conveniences of the city, such as the oil lamps. They seemed to typify the new musical light that was coming into his life as compared with the candle flame of his own home.

Ignace began his lessons at the Conservatory with eager anticipation. But his youthful hopes were abruptly stifled by the discouraging criticism of his first teacher. And this was only one of several disheartening evaluations of the lad's pianistic aptitude. One teacher flatly declared that his hands were not adapted to piano playing. Another advised him, "Do not try to play the piano, because you will *never* be a pianist. Never." Still another teacher with whom he studied the violin would have ended his entire musical career, by saying, "You are not a musician—you have not even a good ear for music, it seems to me. You have absolutely no talent for music. You should stop the lessons now. It's a waste of money." Less stouthearted souls would have wilted under these onslaughts, but the lad with the red and tousled hair had "inner convictions" and a faith in his own future that would not be moved.

Undaunted by his last teacher's ultimatum that he was not to return for further piano lessons, he struggled on alone for a while and prepared a repertory of compositions by Chopin and Liszt. Meanwhile the idea of giving some concerts developed into a definite plan in which Ignace was to be the pianist in a musical troupe. The members, all Conservatory pupils, consisted of a violinist, a cellist, and the sixteen-year-old pianist. In high spirits the trio set out for north Poland and Russia. Love of adventure and the need for money goaded them on.

For a time they met with success and even made a little money on the concerts. But when the cellist decided to part company and return to Warsaw, good fortune also parted with the two remaining recitalists. They met with difficulties on every hand. Their money ran low. For ten days the two lived on a loaf of bread and some tea. They had left Warsaw in summer clothes, and now as the weather became colder they had to cover themselves with newspapers under their vests to keep warm. Then the violinist returned home. Ignace went on alone. He finally arrived at Leningrad, having been gone a year. His father had sent him sufficient funds to return home, so he planned to go directly from Leningrad to his home. Shortly after arriving in the city he met an acquaintance who appeared to be very much interested in his immediate plans. Ignace confided in the young man even to the extent of loaning him all his money. He never saw man or money again. Moreover, when he went to the railroad station for his luggage, it too had been stolen. So for two weeks he tramped the streets of the city like a wandering beggar. Providentially, it seems, his father dreamed of his plight and again sent money for his return home.

Ignace and his father were overwhelmed with joy at seeing each other, and Ignace vowed that he would yet bring happiness to his dear father. And he did. He returned to the Conservatory, and in six months finished his course. His father came to the city for the commencement program, where he saw Ignace receive his diploma and heard him play the Grieg *Concerto*. It was his happy day!

Seated next to the father and sharing his joy at Ignace's graduation and in his brilliant performance of the *Concerto* was another enraptured listener—the youth's sweetheart. She had become a Conservatory student during his senior year. Her sweet and modest ways, her talent, and even her name, Antonina, which was the same as that of his sister, combined to captivate the heart of the handsome young pianist. With love came a new light into his eyes, a new inspiration to dream and to work, a new incentive to pursue a distant goal.

The happy thoughts of the lover found expression in an *Impromptu,* published in Warsaw when he was nineteen. The following year they were married. They began housekeeping in a one-room apartment. Although a member of the Conservatory faculty, the young teacher's piano lessons brought him only twenty-three cents an hour. The couple were poor in material possessions, but rich in hopes for their future and in the happiness of having each other.

But the brilliant burst of happiness was short-lived, for after a year of married life his wife died, leaving him with an infant son. This bitter loss turned all his hopes to despair. His father and dear friends sought to console him, but in spite of their solace, he felt that he was utterly alone. Then as he turned to his piano to give expression to his poignant grief, music, "medicine of the broken heart," brought him comfort and a renewed vision of his musical future.

Although uncertain as to the best course in which to direct his musical art, Paderewski, after placing his child with his grandmother, set out for Berlin for further study. Inasmuch as a number of his teachers had discouraged him in regard to his future as a pianist, and on the other hand he had received much encouragement as a composer, he decided to concentrate on advanced composition. For months he studied arduously, ten to twelve hours a day. Then at a chance meeting with the Russian pianist, Anton Rubinstein, a few encouraging words were spoken by the master that proved to be but the spark to fire the pianistic ambitions of the young aspiring musician. Rubinstein complimented him on his inborn technique, and prophesied for him a "splendid pianistic career."

Paderewski returned to Warsaw and to teaching for a time, but with each passing day his "inner conviction" became stronger. He must leave Warsaw for more serious study of his chosen instrument and then launch out on his career. So he set his face toward Vienna, the European mecca of music, with the celebrated teacher, Leschetizky, the lodestar of his early years, as the particular goal of his pilgrimage.

When at last Paderewski stood in Leschetizky's presence he felt that he had reached a supreme moment in his life. In response to the professor's request that he demonstrate his pianistic ability, the twenty-four-year-old student chose several of his own compositions. As he played, the old master observed him critically. Paderewski breathlessly awaited his verdict. Then, as if Leschetisky were seeking to climax all the unfavorable criticisms of the young man's earlier teachers, he uttered the fateful words, "Too late!" Paderewski was almost stunned by the impact of the verdict.

Then Leschetizky explained to the younger musician that although he had enormous talent the most precious years of his life had been wasted in misdirected practice. He told him further that he had not yet learned *how to work,* which was particularly noticeable in his undisciplined fingering. However, he accepted Paderewski as a pupil, and together they worked with intensive devotion, as if seeking to retrieve a lost career. Their method of procedure was so meticulous in every detail, and so rigorous in its discipline that "on the education of every finger," in the words of the English critic Raymond, "was lavished as much pains as go to the instruction of the children of a good-sized township. The most repellent labor was faced, the most alluring temptations set aside, in order that the very maximum of digital dexterity—the rest was in the man's soul —should be obtained. . . . The skill was largely a matter of sheer hard work, of self-discipline exceeding that of most old saints, of a savage energy which in another orbit might have guided half a dozen trusts." The experience of age and the energy of youth joined their efforts in a common purpose until they had erected an enduring pianistic superstructure on the ruins of a faulty technique.

The reward of conquest came when Leschetizky suggested that Paderewski make his debut in Vienna. The recital was a tremendous success, and the young artist was engaged for recitals in other places, including Paris. There he was heard by several noted French orchestral conductors, who were so enthusiastic about his performance that one of them offered the young man an opportunity to play with the orchestra.

Paderewski returned to Vienna, and to Leschetizky, with the ovation of Paris still ringing in his ears. He came back, not to glory in his success, but to work. He realized that his toil was not over; it had just begun. His concert repertory covered only one program; he must enlarge it. He knew now that his name was rising on the musical horizon. He must meet the challenge.

Swiftly the fame of the golden-maned Pole spread over the Continent and to other shores. He crossed the channel into England, where the critics at first received his playing with apathy and even derision. G. Bernard Shaw described him as "an immensely spirited young, harmonious blacksmith, who puts a concerto on the piano as upon an anvil and hammers it out with an exuberant enjoyment of the swing and strength of the proceeding. . . . His concerto was over, the audience in a wild enthusiasm, and the pianoforte a wreck." Throughout his training the young pianist had become accustomed to adverse criticisms, and now as heretofore they were accepted as challenges that must be met and conquered. In time he won the acclaim of all England, from the lowliest music lover, standing in a preconcert queue, to Queen Victoria on her throne.

Though the laudations of the Old World brought gratification to the artist, he regarded them, not as laurels of ease, but as vanes indicating that he was now headed in the right direction. There was a new world to conquer. America was beckoning! A tour of eighty concerts was arranged, and in November, 1891, Paderewski boarded the steamer The Spray for the "land of promise."

His first concert, together with orchestra, was given at Carnegie Hall, in New York City. He played the *Concerto in G minor,* by Saint-Saens, a group of Chopin solos, and his own *Concerto in A minor,* Opus 17, Number 1. The music critics varied in their appraisals, from disapprobation to enthusiastic commendation.

The New York debut was important apart from the particular merits of the performance in that it initiated in America one of the most fabulous careers in the history of music. The pianist appeared in eighteen concerts in New York City the first season. For forty years thereafter he traversed the highways and byways of the earth, making plain to multitudes the deeper beauties of noble music. In America alone he played personally before five million people. His tours, made in a private railroad car, reached into every State of the Union and into the provinces of Canada. He concertized in South America, Africa, and Australia. His name became a household word. What would the teachers of his early days have thought if they had witnessed his success?

Concertgoers who had the privilege of hearing Paderewski in recital were rewarded with a unique experience. As he made his appearance on the stage, it seemed that a figure from the Romantic Era had stepped into the present, that the days of Chopin and Liszt had returned. There was a blend of graciousness, dignity, and sincerity in his bearing as he bowed to the applause of an audience that, as one man, had risen to its feet. The resounding opening chords, used as a prelude to his program, emanated from the twilight of the stage as a stentorian declaration of what was to come. He then proceeded to recreate the inmost thoughts of the masters and to make them living and "interesting to all classes of hearers." For three hours and more he would regale his listeners with the interpretations of a tone poet, the musical colors of a tone painter, and the clean-cut rhetorical divisions of a musical orator.

The master pianist's playing was noteworthy for its singing-tone quality, so essential as a medium of interpretation in the soulful styles, such as the Chopin nocturnes; for its flexible rubato, vitalizing the rhythmic pulse of the Polish dance forms —the mazurkas and the polonaises; for a sparklingly clean virtuosity as displayed in his version of *La Campanella*, by Paganini-Liszt, and similar styles.

Although these artistic attributes stamped Paderewski's playing with an individuality that set it apart from that of his contemporaries, there was, beyond these, a philosophy of noble living, a sense of spiritual values, that gave his musical message a universal appeal. Behind his penetrating interpretations was a life experience. He had partaken of an overflowing cup of human grief, and he had shared in life's purest joys.

He had learned the important lesson of humility. He brought this same humble approach to his interpretations of the masters. His modest attitude is illustrated by a story often told:

An American girl, visiting Beethoven's home, approached his piano, sat down, and indifferently strummed a light tune. Her conversation with the custodian, as related by Charles Phillips, was as follows:

"I suppose you have many visitors here?" the girl inquired.

"Yes, a great many."

"Many famous people, no doubt."

"Yes. Paderewski came recently."

"I suppose he played on this piano?" and her fingers ran a scale on the keys.

"No, Paderewski did not consider himself worthy to play on Beethoven's piano."

His bountiful heart overflowed in many kind and generous deeds. When visiting the home of Andrew Carnegie, the latter's old colored servant stumbled down a stairway while carrying a hot drink to serve Mr. Paderewski. The drink scalded the negro's face and eyes, and as a result he became nearly blind. Paderewski tenderly cared for the old man as long as he was a guest in the home, and as a parting gesture of his genuine solicitude, arranged for the purchase of a farm in Georgia, native State of the servant. He presented the property deed to the servant, thereby providing for his security and comfort for the rest of his days.

Suffering and grief have produced beautiful music. Paderewski knew these at first hand, and they contributed toward the deep-dyed coloring of his interpretations. A few years after the death of his wife, his infant son became afflicted with infantile paralysis, and had to spend the remainder of his life in a wheel chair until his death at twenty. Alfred, handsome and gifted, was the pride of his father's life, and to see him stricken was one of the heaviest crosses he had to bear. But even this cross led to a crown. From the tender motherly care of the boy's nurse, love bloomed, and in 1899 she and the father were married in Warsaw. Through the changing years she poured the balm of selfless devotion on the troublous experiences that beset the path of the concert artist.

Paderewski's music covered a wide range of expression because he had drunk deep draughts of life's bitter and sweet waters. His music was lofty because it reflected his strong character, his humanity, his integrity. His own life, unspoiled by adulation and refined by adversity, in turn lifted other lives through the medium of music. The American poet John H. Finley, addressing the master, said:

> "Your touch has been transmuted into sound
> As perfect as an orchid or a rose,
> True as a mathematic formula
> Yet full of color as an evening sky.
> But there's a symphony that you've evoked
> From out the hearts of men, more wonderful
> Than you have played upon your instrument."

While the name of Ignace Paderewski is generally associated with the interpretation of piano music, his creative utterances, comprising all forms, were considerable. His popular *Minuet* is a mere trifle in comparison with the large group of works of high merit that came from his pen. The *Minuet*, incidentally the outgrowth of a little joke, became his most famous composition.

During his Warsaw days Paderewski, then twenty-six, used to visit a physician-friend occasionally. The old doctor was a lover of music, especially the music of Mozart, and whenever Paderewski would visit him, he would request a number by Mozart. As the young pianist's Mozart repertory was limited, and as he was yet not far removed from his prankster days, he decided to have a little fun at his host's expense. So before his next visit he improvised a dance in the style of Mozart. Then when he arrived at his friend's house and again was requested to play some Mozart, he played his new composition, the "Minuet." "O Mozart!" cried his host. "What a wonderful piece! Tell me, Paderewski, is there anyone now alive who could write such music?" Thereupon the pianist explained that he himself had composed the "Minuet" as a surprise, a little joke. The jest has been well-nigh forgotten, but the "Minuet" lives on.

His larger creations include an opera, *Manru; Symphony in B minor; Piano Concerto in A minor; Polish Fantasy on Original Themes for Piano and Orchestra;* many sets of piano pieces, such as *Chant du Voyageur,* Opus 8, which includes the much-loved "Melody in B major"; and *Humoresques,* of which "Cracovienne Fantastique" is the most popular. His lyric style is represented in several groups of songs. In all there were twenty-four published opus numbers, a very large output, when one considers the time consumed by his extensive concert tours.

The musical dreams of Paderewski's boyhood were being abundantly realized. He had risen from achievement to achievement, from honor to honor. Now in command of his full-winged flight toward the zenith of his career, he suddenly swerved in his course when a signal of distress arose from his native land as millions of his countrymen were precipitated into war. The hour of his second dream, the restoration of his people had come. With dramatic swiftness he was to change from the role of an artist to that of a statesman. He was to forsake the mastery of one instrument for that of a greater one. He was to play on human heartstrings; he was to direct a symphony of life.

Paderewski's villa near Morges, Switzerland, which was to

be the scene of the master's metamorphosis, had, since the early part of the century, afforded him a retreat from the rigors of his concert tours. Here, as gardener and farmer, he had found relaxation from the exacting strain of his long journeys. His love of nature was satisfied as he tended the cherry orchard, the rose garden, and the grape vines on his sixty-acre estate. Domestic and imported birds, pure-bred horses, prize-winning sheep, a dozen dogs, and other animals made up the menagerie which yielded him many delightful hours. His love of people attracted visitors of all classes, from little children of the neighboring regions to artists and statesmen from afar.

The thirty-first of July, Paderewski's name day, was always a gala occasion in the master's household. Visitors from many lands came to honor and renew friendships with the genial host. Delicious foods were served; there were games and fire-work displays. There were musical fireworks too, as one celebrated musician after another contributed his share of the entertainment.

The festive occasion was celebrated, as usual, in 1914. Fanciful decorations, consisting of Chinese lanterns, festoons, and paper dragons, created an Oriental atmosphere about the house and lawns. The clear Alpine skies looked down upon a scene of tranquil beauty. The grand majesty of the Swiss mountain ranges, white peaked, invulnerable, lent a feeling of security to the villa and the surrounding countryside; the blue waters of Lake Geneva lent an atmosphere of serene enchantment.

Inside the rambling house the guests, all garbed in Oriental costumes, had been having a hilarious evening. The hour was approaching midnight and the festivities were at their height when suddenly a message came over the wires that startled the gathering into a solemn silence. War had come to Europe!

Paderewski could read the handwriting on the wall. He knew that his country would soon be devastated. Perhaps, thought he, out of this ravished land there would rise a new Poland, a people freed from the enslaving shackles that had been forged for a century and a half. To this cause and to the relief of his already stricken people he dedicated his life and fortune. As he had brought the beauty and balm of music to many the world over, he now resolved to bring hope and succor to his own kin.

The world was not long in realizing that Paderewski's genius extended beyond the realm of music. He became recognized as a courageous, clear-eyed leader. His first act, after evaluating the needs arising from the inroads already made by the war, was to organize a relief committee. Shortly afterward he sailed for England and America, to acquaint these great nations with the dire fate of his people. In contrast with former tours in which, as a conquering musical hero he had received the plaudits of multitudes, he now came as a "beggar" in the cause of his brethren. Evincing an eloquence of oratory on a plane with that of his music, he created goodwill everywhere and received a generous response to his mission of mercy.

Beyond this immediate goal there was ever present in Pad-erewski's mind that greater goal, which he had envisioned since his boyhood, the liberation of Poland. To this worthy end he now bent all the energy and resourcefulness of his being. He selected America, cradle of liberty, as the field of strategy. Here his personality and gift of friendliness enabled him to form a chain of friendships which ultimately led to audiences with the great leaders of the nation, including the Secretary of State; Colonel House, a Presidential adviser; and finally to President Wilson himself.

Mr. Paderewski pleaded so eloquently for the Polish cause that he won the wholehearted support of the American states-men. From these significant contacts the scope of his influence widened until it reached the halls of Congress and the Peace Conference. It was felt in the thirteenth of Wilson's Fourteen Points, wherein, referring to Poland, "economic independence and territorial integrity should be guaranteed by international agreement."

That Paderewski's qualities of leadership should mark him for a position of greater responsibility in the rehabilitation of

Poland was inevitable. When he arrived in Poland during December of 1918, he was given a triumphal welcome by a people enjoying the first taste of liberation, the first fruits of his years of unselfish service. To hundreds of thousands in great cities and small, he was more than a master pianist or an ardent patriot. He was a deliverer.

During the month of January, 1919, Paderewski was appointed prime minister and minister of foreign affairs in the newly formed coalition government. In this capacity he was a delegate to the Peace Conference. Colonel House, speaking of Paderewski's new role, said:

"Those associated with Paderewski during the stirring days from the time of our entrance into the war until the Peace Conference had finished its labors, saw a new and unfamiliar Paderewski. The artist, the composer, the poetic dreamer had left no trace of himself. The old personality had been submerged in the new, and we saw the orator, the executive, the man of action." Secretary of State Lansing was impressed that "Ignace Paderewski was a greater statesman than he was musician, that he was an able and tactful leader of his countrymen and a sagacious diplomat." Secretary of the Interior Franklin K. Lane, in discussing the Polish leader, said, "He is the outstanding phenomenon of the war."

After the signing of the Versailles Treaty the Polish prime minister returned to his native land, concerned about the difficult problems associated with unifying and providing relief for his people. As he grappled with the weighty affairs of government he never allowed himself to deviate from principles of right and justice. He was ever the embodiment of integrity. "It has been my privilege to fathom the man," wrote Colonel House, "and to look into the windows of a great soul. I have never found him guilty of an unworthy act." The breadth of his vision and his wholesome, unselfish attitude were never more clearly revealed than when, faced with a decision between self-interests and the welfare of his people, he chose the latter. As prejudice and persecution arose against him in certain quarters, rather than assume dictatorial powers to crush out opposition, he laid aside the mantle of office, his record unstained, his conscience free. He had sacrificed his fortune and five years of his musical career for the sake of his motherland.

Although past sixty, Paderewski returned to his first love, music, relinquishing all purely political positions for that of musical ambassador-at-large to the world. He was still a favorite son of Poland, but his music belonged to all mankind. His music now was embued with a new depth of feeling; it had grown ripe in the vicissitudes of life's victories and defeats; it had become vibrant with the pulse of his kinsmen.

The road over which Paderewski had traveled from obscurity to world eminence had been long, rugged, and often lonely. He had passed through valleys of sorrow and pain; he had been beset by voices from the wilderness of doubt and prejudice. And ever as he went he scattered the myrrh of music, gave bread to the hungry, and by courageous leadership brought deliverance to those who were oppressed. Now, in his life's sunset, having reached the summit of his career, he was not content to view his accomplishments in self-ease and self-satisfaction. In spite of the infirmities of age he continued to spend himself in making the lives of others rich and full and free.

It was late June, 1941. In a New York City apartment an old man and his sister were quietly reminiscing about their childhood days. They talked of their youth and the intervening years. They talked of his extensive and devoted service in the cause of music. Their thoughts wandered, unchecked, down the corridors of the years.

The master's musical career had reached its closing hour, solemn and tender, like a soft afterglow to his colorful life. The moments, now lingering, now fleeting, seemed to evoke the lines of the blind artist, E. B. Perry:

> "For what the gain of all my toilsome years,
> Of all my ceaseless struggles, ceaseless tears?
> My best, more brief than frailest summer flowers,
> Dies with the hour.

"Mine but the task to lift, a little space,
The mystic veil from beauty's radiant face
That other men may joy thereon to see,
Forgetting me.

"The Artist passes like a swift-blown breeze,
Or vapors floating up from summer seas;
But Art endures as long as life and love:
For her I strove."

Their reflections turned to the old country. They became sad when they spoke of their beloved homeland, for Poland, which for a time had been free, was now under bondage again. As the man of fourscore years, who had done so much for his country, arose from his bed he slowly repeated the words of a fellow patriot, "I am dying too soon. . . . How sad, for I shall not see a free Poland!" He stepped feebly to the piano, and gathering together all his remaining strength, played the Polish National Anthem. This was his farewell to the two loves of his long life —*music* and *country*.

The world remembers Ignace Jan Paderewski in the measure of a great artist-pianist, composer, and musical patriot. The world remembers him, moreover, in the measure of a great man. The strength of his music was rooted in the strength of his character. The breadth of his influence in art and statecraft stemmed from unblemished motives. "His heart is pure, his life clean, his ideals lofty," wrote one author, and therein expressed the Polish master's birthright to true and abiding greatness.

Jean Sibelius

1865-

I will sing the people's legends,
And the ballads of the nation.
                              —The Kalevala.

W ORLD WAR I had reached its darkest hour!
Finland's musical envoy to the world sat with bowed head
in his study at Villa Ainola, near Jarvenpaa. A sense of the futility of mankind's recurring outbursts of violence toward one
another, concern for the fate of his country, and apprehension
for the welfare of his home and family weighed heavily on the
composer's heart. A sharp knock brought him to his feet. At the
door a soldier from the Red army curtly informed him that he was
no longer at liberty to leave his home. The soldier turned abruptly
and stamped away into the February snowstorm, leaving the
bewildered composer to ponder his fate as a homebound prisoner.
Sibelius understood the import of the mission. He knew that
even the military recognized the potency of patriotically inspired
music such as he wrote.

Bolder invasions of his home were subsequently made. Once
while a mob of soldiers was engaged in looting the sacred pre-
cincts of his home, the composer strode majestically, though
nervously, to the piano and played invincible music, music that

calmed his terrified children and evoked the admiration of the rough guards.

In time the master was given permission to leave his home for a safer haven. Reluctantly he turned his back on his white log house and left for Helsinki, where he found refuge in his physician-brother's hospital. The institution was in the hands of the Russians, so the Sibelius family spent some extremely trying days under the same roof with the rough and ravenous soldiers, whose needs were given precedence over those of the native civilians. In a few weeks the master lost forty pounds in weight. But he fed his soul on noble though somber thoughts, buoyed by the courage of his compatriots and by the certain knowledge that when the fury of battle would be spent, Finland would emerge a stronger and more united people.

Then slowly but surely the clouds of war lifted; the Russians had been routed from the capital, and Finland was free. When once again the master viewed the countryside about his villa kissed by the dew of peace, his soul was refreshed. He had emerged from the scene of combat triumphant in spirit, ready to impart new strength and serenity to his music.

Sibelius laid plans for another symphony—his seventh. The complex patterns and broad lines of a symphonic masterpiece represent the culmination of a master's natural and cultivated endowments. He weaves into its fabric the patterns of his own character and life. The threads of Sibelius' *Seventh Symphony* had been spun a half century earlier in the character and habits that were built into the home life of his childhood.

Musical fortune smiled and breathed a blessing at Jean's birth. He was favored not only with natural gifts beyond that given to most mortals but with the requisite character and self-discipline necessary to perfect and polish the thought gems that would course through his mind. Jean's father, a physician at Tavastehus, was beloved in all the community for his friendliness and kind deeds. Dr. Sibelius was Swedish on his mother's side, so Jean came of mixed Swedish-Finnish blood. Both parents loved music and were musically talented.

The Sibelius home was thrice blessed in well-favored, talented children. A daughter, Linda, was the first born. After two years the lusty squalls of a bouncing boy brought joy to the doctor's heart. Soon the entire community had heard about Jean, and all rejoiced in the stories about him from the lips of the proud father as he made his calls among them. When, several years later, another son, Christian, was born, it seemed their cup of gladness was nearly full.

Then tragedy struck! Famine, accompanied by typhus and death, swept over the land. Dr. Sibelius worked untiringly to check the scourge in his community. But in saving others he sacrificed himself to the dread disease—famine fever.

Indulgent relatives contributed their share toward charting the course of the youngster's lives. Jean developed a marked attachment for his uncles, and the fact that his life conformed to certain standards and patterns is directly traceable to their influence. Uncle Johan had died before Jean's birth, but at least in one particular he made his imprint on the future of his nephew. A sea captain, Uncle Johan had left on a voyage to Havana, Cuba. It proved to be his last. In his effects was found a stack of visiting cards on each of which the name Jean Sibelius had been printed. Years later when Jean (he had been christened Janne) found them he liked the French rendering of the name so well that he adopted it for his own. Uncle Pehr was a businessman in Abo. Jean and Uncle Pehr were fond of each other, and both loved music passionately. Why the good uncle's whimsical nature dictated that he should begin playing his violin at two o'clock in the morning seems incomprehensible except as an eccentric trait that showed itself variously in the Sibelius line.

In most ways Jean was a typical boy. He was robust, jolly, and carefree. He was exceptionally kind. At one time he was given some money to make a purchase of books. On the way he met a poor beggar woman, whose pleadings so touched the boy that he gave her all the money he had. The books had to wait until another day.

He enjoyed the outdoors and reveled in walks through the woods at dusk, when his lively imagination made living creatures out of every shadowy form. "When one saw him in the country," wrote Arvid Jarnefelt, "even if it were in a meadow, he was able to live his own full life even there: a bird twitters —he pricks up his ears—a shepherdess calls—the melody enters his soul forever. He absorbed everything that each passing hour caused to bloom, all that reached his ear, that his eye beheld. He lived every moment so intensively that at times he really recalled an animal, a fish jumping in a rapid, or a young hunting dog that gasps for breath as it scents game—or a bird that, even when sitting still, turns its head in order to hear every rustle and to catch all that living reality has to tell it."

His music lessons began at nine, although already at five he had shown musical talent. He loathed his lessons. In the schoolroom he was unconformable as a pupil; his mind was keen and imaginative, but he was continually in a world of dreams. He dreamed first and foremost of becoming a violin virtuoso. He often strode through the forest and played to the birds or stood in a boat on the water and "improvised to the sea." He listened to nature's own music, the call of the birds, gurgling rivulets, the play of the wind in the trees, and then reproduced these effects through the voice of music. It seemed that nearly everything he saw or heard turned to music. He was a born painter in tones. The various tonalities were the colors on his palette. A friend of his youth tells of a conversation with him during which Jean juggled "with colors and sounds as if they were bright glass balls, made colors resound and sounds glow so that A major became blue and C major red, F major green and D major yellow."

As much as music was honored and loved all down the Sibelius line, they held to the conventional idea regarding music as an honorable career. Music was lovely enough as a pleasurable pastime, but in the serious business of choosing a vocation it was not to be considered. So it came about that Jean, against his own wish, reached Helsinki at the age of nineteen to study law. Schumann and Tchaikovsky had also launched out on a law career. Fortunately they had veered from their course. Jean began to study in earnest. But as with Robert and Peter Ilich, though he stared into tomes on law and economics, his mind wandered into the forbidden bypaths of natural and musical sound. When he opened the window and breathed the fresh incense arising from the flowers and trees, his longing to express his appreciation through music became intense. One day he left his open law book on the window sill, and there it lay undisturbed for weeks while Jean played his violin and composed. When an uncle paid him a surprise visit he soon discovered the telltale evidence on the window sill. His uncle drew a deep sigh. "After all, Janne," he began, while the youth breathlessly waited every word, "it would be best for you to devote yourself entirely to music, seeing that study does not interest you any more than this." We know not what jurisprudence lost when he closed its books forever, but we do know by his choosing music as a career he has brought honor and resourcefulness to music.

Just at this time Jean had the good fortune to become acquainted with the head of the musical academy, who proved himself a great teacher and a true friend. Jean came to confide in the older man, and together they drew the pattern for the boy's dawning career. Wegelius was somehow able to pierce the shell of reticence about the lad and to lead him to liberate his feelings to the world.

An introduction to the Jarnefelt family brought a new circle of influence around the young musician that would widen with the years. The father, a lieutenant-general with a colorful career, was intensely patriotic. There were three sons, all in the process of choosing their careers of art and letters, in which they were to become notably distinguished. There was one daughter named after one of the characters in *Kalevala*, Aino, toward whom Jean at first cast shy glances, and who eventually became the consuming love of his life and the bride for which Villa Ainola was named.

It was at the Jarnefelt home that Jean listened to animated patriotic discussions that fanned into a white flame his ardor for Finlandia's legends and heroes and countryside. As Jean's love of nature matured it grew into a passionate love for his country that became the dominating urge behind his indefatigable creative faculty. The abundance of works based on Finland's lore and legends that would in time come from his pen attest to that absorbing vision that was given its initial impetus at the Jarnefelt residence. Important compositions such as the following tone poems and suites are based on the *Kalevala: Karelia Suite; The Swan of Tuonela; Pohjola's Daughter; The Bard.*

The *Kalevala* is the Finnish national epic. Longfellow conceived his Hiawatha after having read a translation of this work. The meter is identical, as are some of the characters and episodes, with the difference that Longfellow transfers them to an Indian setting. Moreover, *Hiawatha* does not reach the degree of fantasy that is reached in the *Kalevala.*

Sibelius was now twenty-four. The rich treasures contained in the *Kalevala* and other national poetry brought fresh draughts of musical ideas to his mind, but the young composer felt that he was inadequately equipped technically and theoretically, to give his thoughts complete expression. So he was drawn to that mecca of musical learning and culture—Germany. On the support of a small scholarship and in company with a few friends, he left the Finnish capital on the steamer *Grand Duke* for Berlin. There he studied under Albert Becker, and found rapturous delight in partaking of the concert season, hearing great orchestral and chamber music, and meeting musical celebrities such as Richard Strauss and Joseph Joachim.

Notwithstanding his crowded hours and his keen interest in the musical activities of the city, there was a constant tugging at his heart for home that increased in intensity as the season came to a close. And when he listened to Finnish music, picturing to him the lakes and forests of his own country, his longing for home became well-nigh overwhelming.

When at last the steamer on which Sibelius was a passenger arrived at Helsinki, the lighthearted youth scampered down the gangplank, toward home and then on to the Jarnefelts.

Jean and Aino spent many happy hours together during that summer. He gained her consent to marry him, and they dreamed of their future together. But before they could culminate their troth, he had to complete his apprenticeship with an older music master. He sought out Wegelius, and they decided that Jean should next go to Vienna. There he spent the following season, coming under the inspiration of Hans Richter, distinguished conductor; Karl Goldmark, composer of the *Golden Wedding Symphony* and the opera *The Queen of Sheba;* and meeting the greatest of living composers, Brahms.

He returned to a Finland seething under oppressive laws imposed by Russia. He joined in with the patriotic movement and became thoroughly imbued with national feeling. As he breathed the stifling atmosphere of tyranny, his mind filled with musical ideas which would inspire his fellow men to throw off the yoke and be free.

Though busy and concerned with establishing himself, the youth found time and thought for love. In the early part of June, 1892, Jean and his fiancee were married and left for a honeymoon of several weeks in the land of Kalevala. Jean doubtless was reminded of the lines in the *Kalevala* which read:

> "You shall have my sister Aino,
> She shall dust your chamber for you,
> And shall wash your garments for you;
> Golden fabrics she shall weave you,
> And shall bake you cakes of honey."

The couple returned to Helsinki and the joys and problems of married life, where for a time Sibelius necessarily wrote bread-and-butter notes. But more and more he was coming into his own as a recognized master. He was the slow-maturing, conscientious, austere, and meticulous type of artist. His *First Symphony in E minor* was given its initial performance in 1899, when the composer was thirty-four. Since then he has consistently devoted much of his genius to orchestral music. Up to the present, seven symphonies have been published and the eighth, in the process of creation for many years, is rumored completed but will not be released for some time—possibly posthumously.

The world beholds with growing wonder the stupendous output of his pen, more remarkable in the light of the knowledge that his first symphony was written comparatively late in life. The possibilities in symphonic music are unlimited. The symphony orchestra consists of an aggregation of instrumental families which merge into a single glorious instrument, infinite in range and timbre, eloquent in every conceivable variety of expression. What a grand instrument in the creative hands of a Beethoven, a Wagner, or a Sibelius. The remarkable effects attained range from the grotesque to the sublime, from the tenderly real to the apparitional.

Sibelius is now rated as one of the greatest symphonists of our time, but he also wrote music that was human, music that would strike a response in the minds of the masses. His *Finlandia*, published about the same time as his *First Symphony*, is such a work. Its intensely patriotic vein stirred to the depths the Finnish people's love for their homeland. It swept across the borders of other lands and became to many their first revelation that there existed a small, honest, and very literate country called Finland.

In 1904 Sibelius purchased a house in the country at Tomasby, atop a hill and near a lake. The composer here had the villa built in which he has spent most of his days since. He has left the Villa Ainola only on rare occasions. He visited France, Italy, and also America, and received the homage that was due him as a visiting musical monarch. He naturally appreciated that his music was being accepted and understood. But with characteristic diffidence he has shrunk from the acclaim that the world has been wont to lay at his feet. He has chosen rather the quiet and peace of his villa, where, unmolested, he might devote his every energy to more completely and perfectly express the mighty musical thoughts that surge unremittingly through his mind.

The solitude which the master craves for work imposes a

similar quiet atmosphere about the entire household. One can imagine, in a home of five daughters, the self-discipline each must exercise in order to stifle all noises, singing or whistling in order that the utmost quiet might be maintained. The privilege of living with a master may be a choice one, but it is also a costly one. The master, we are told by Mme. Sibelius, is so little concerned with the things of this world that he consults neither watch nor clock, and often does not stop to learn what day of the week it may be or "even whether it is night or day." In order to be a great master, a man must sacrifice many of the ordinary joys of life for the privilege of living close to the dwelling place of Inspiration. Does not the greater privilege, lie in the precious heritage afforded any and all who appropriate the perfected works of their hands?

When Sibelius reached seventy, the world paused to pay him tribute in glowing words. Lawrence Gilman, spoke of Sibelius as "the most original of living music makers, the most original and detached—one who stands aside from the contemporary tonal pageant, unaffected by its tumult and its shouting; watching gravely, as from a distance, its caperings and its shows, content to produce the noblest and loftiest music of our time."

More than a decade has passed since these words were broadcast to the world. Sibelius' search for the good and true and beautiful goes on. Neighbors of the family have told of seeing the master at his desk, writing music far into the night until the two tall candles at his elbows burned into the holder sockets.

Perchance some of these neighbors who have known the great composer since the vigor of his manhood may be reminded by the low-burning candles that even the great light that was his is waxing dim, and that shadows are playing about. But as Finland and the music-loving, freedom-loving, world ponders his close of day, there appears the picture of a golden, glorious sunset.